HUGO'S
PORTUGUESE
PHRASE BOOK

D0945850

Published by

Hugo's Language Books Limited

104 JUDD STREET, LONDON WC1H 9NF

Translation and pronunciation by
Manolo Santos
Series editor: R. Batchelor-Smith

Contents

Introduction

This is primarily a phrase book in which selections of everyday words and phrases, complete with imitated pronunciation, are grouped under the usual headings of "Hotels and Accommodation", "Motoring", "Shopping" and so on. There are also conversion tables for weights, measures, distances, tyre pressures and clothing sizes.

In addition to the general notes that accompany each heading, there is more detailed information on Portuguese history, the people, social habits and customs, and the language. It sometimes happens that the tourist, despite his excellent intentions, causes both himself and his host unnecessary embarrassment by committing some innocent breach of local custom or etiquette. We hope that this book will enable you to avoid making such mistakes, as well as helping you to make yourself understood.

It is a good idea to read through everything beforehand; as you become familiar with the book's scope, you will see that many phrases can be combined and interchanged in order to meet almost any situation.

THE LANGUAGE, IMITATED PRONUNCIATION

Given the complex sound structure of Portuguese it is not always possible to transcribe its pronunciation in terms of English spelling. Nonetheless, the "key" and notes that follow should enable the English reader to master with ease the most elusive as well as the most obvious Portuguese sounds, and so to understand and make himself understood in Portugal.

When reading the imitated pronunciation, avoid pauses between the syllables. Pronounce these as if they formed part of an English word, always emphasizing the one printed in bold type—the stressed syllable—which in Portuguese is often marked by one of the written accents: acute (á), grave (à), circumflex (â).

Consonants

You should have no trouble with **b, d, f, l, p, q, t** and **v**; these are all pronounced as in English. The others vary, and are explained below. The right-hand column shows how each letter is written in the imitated pronunciation, and examples follow each explanation.

c	(1) before a, o, u: like *k* in *kipper*.	*k*
	capa = **kah**-*per*	
	(2) before e, i: like *s* in *soap*.	*s*
	cinco = **seen**^{g}-*k^{oo}*	

ç	only used before a, o, u: like *s* in *soap*. açucar = *er*-**soo**-*ker*	s
ch	always before a vowel: like *sh* in *shot*. chuva = **shoo**-*ver*	sh
g	(1) before e, i: like *s* in *measure*. gente = **zhe**(y)n*ᵍ*-*tᵉ*	zh
	(2) elsewhere: like *g* in *gulp*. garfo = **ghahr**-*fᵒᵒ*	gh
h	always silent.	
j	only used before a vowel: like *s* in *measure*. janela = *zher*-**neh**-*ler*	zh
lh	similar to *ll* in *million* (press tongue against palate and utter *l*). alho = **ah**-*llᵒᵒ*	ll
m	(1) initial m, or between two vowels, or after a consonant: as in English. calma = **kahl**-*mer*	m
	(2) before b or p, or at the end of a word, it is not pronounced as a distinct consonant. It indicates a nasal sound on the preceding vowel. (See Nasal Vowels, page 12). sombra = **sohn**ᵍ-*brer*	nᵍ
n	(1) at the beginning of a word, or between two vowels, or after a consonant: as in English. nadar = *ner*-**dahr**	n

7

	(2) before d or t it is not pronounced as a distinct consonant, but indicates a nasal sound on the preceding vowel (see page 12). ontem = **ohn**^{g}-*tehn*^{g}	n^g
nh	similar to *n* in *onion* (press tongue against palate and utter n). vinho = **vee**-*nn*^{oo}	*nn*
r	rolled as in the Scottish accent. cara = **kah**-*rer*	*r*
rr	used only between vowels, it may be emphatically trilled or pronounced as the French r. carro = **kah**-*rr*^{oo}	*rr*
s	(1) as an initial s, or after a consonant, it is like the *s* in *salt*. sol = *sohl*	*s*
	(2) between two vowels: like an emphatic English *z*. casa = **kah**-*zer*	*z*
	(3) at the end of a word or before a consonant: like *s* in *sugar*. cisne = **seesh**-*n*^{e}	*sh*
x	(1) as an initial x: like *sh* in *shoe*. xadrez = **sher**-**dre(y)sh**	*sh*
	(2) between vowels: sometimes like *s* in *salt*. próximo = **proh**-*see*-*m*^{oo}	*s*

8

(3) in words of learned derivation: like *x* in *annexe*.   **ks**

reflexo = **rr**ᵉ**-fleh**-*ks*ᵒᵒ

(4) in the prefix ex- before a vowel: like the English *z*.   **z**

exército = *i*-**zehr**-*see*-*t*ᵒᵒ

(5) in the prefix ex- before a consonant: similar to the English *sh*.   **sh**

êxtase = **aysh**-*ter*-*z*ᵉ

z

(1) at the beginning of a word or between vowels: like *z* in *zone*.   **z**

zero = **zeh**-*r*ᵒᵒ; exemplo = *i*-**ze(y)n**ᵍ-*pl*ᵒᵒ

(2) at the end of a word it is always like *sh* in *shell*.   **sh**

voz = *vohsh*

Vowels

Note that the Portuguese vowels are classified as "open", "close", "muted" or "neutral"; this refers to the position of the lips when sounding them.

á, à, a

(1) Open: when stressed, is similar to *a* in *father*.   **ah**

pato = **pah**-*t*ᵒᵒ

â, a

(2) Close: when stressed, at the end of a word, or before m, n or nh, it is like *er* in *mother*.   **er**

ama = **er**-*mer*

9

é, e	(1) Open: when stressed, like *e* in *egg*. panela = per-**neh**-ler	*eh*
ê, e	(2) Close: when stressed, similar to *ey* in *they*, without the final y. cabelo = ker-**be(y)**-l^{oo}	*e(y)*
e	(3) Neutral: like the neutral sound of the second *e* in *general*, when unstressed, and becoming very faint at the end of a word. norte = **norh**-t^e	*e*
	(4) Similar to *i*, as the first syllable, before a and o, and as the conjunction **e** (and). edificio = i-d^e-**fee**-see-^{oo}	*i*
e(x)	(5) When in the prefix ex-, it is similar to *a* in *late*. expiar = aysh-pee-**ahr**	*ay*
í, i	(1) Open: when stressed, like *ee* in *sheep* menino = m^e-**nee**-n^{oo}	*ee*
i	(2) Close: when unstressed, like *i* in *ticket*. igual = i-**ghwahl**	*i*
ó, o	(1) Open: when stressed, like *o* in *rock*. obra = **oh**-brer	*oh*
ô, o	(2) Close: when stressed, like *ou* in *poultry*. boca = **bou**-ker	*ou*
o	(3) Neutral: unstressed and becoming very faint at the end of a word. dormir = d^{oo}r-**meer**	*oo*

10

ú, u	(1) Stressed, is like *oo* in *book*.	*oo*
	puro = **poo**-*r⁰⁰*	
u	(2) Unstressed, is also like *oo* in *book*.	
	unir = *oo*-**neer**	*oo*
	(3) Silent: in gu and qu before e or i.	
	quente = **ke(y)n**ᵍ-*tᵉ*	

Oral diphthongs

These are single vowel sounds that result from the combination of the oral vowels a, e, o, u with a following i or u (the stress falling generally on the first vowel), or with a preceding gu or qu – in cases where the u is voiced, such as **agua** and **igual**. Not all the oral diphthongs can be transcribed into English, as will be seen below.

ai	Open: as *ie* in *tie*; pai = *pahi*	*ahi*
au	Open: as *ow* in *cow*; mau = *mah⁰⁰*	*ah⁰⁰*
ei	Close: as *ey* in *they*; peito = **pe(y)i**-*t⁰⁰*	*e(y)i*
eu	Open; chapéu = *sher*-**peh⁰⁰**	*eh⁰⁰*
eu	Close; meu = *me(y)⁰⁰*	*e(y)⁰⁰*
iu	Open; fugiu = *foo*-**zhi⁰⁰**	*ee⁰⁰*
oi	Open: as *oi* in *noise*;	*ohi*
	comboio = *kohn*ᵍ-**bohi**-*⁰⁰*	
oi	Close: noite = **noui**-*tᵉ*	*oui*
ou	Close: ouvido = *ou*-**vee**-*d⁰⁰*	*ou*
ui	Close: similar to *ui* in *nuisance*, if one	*⁰⁰i*
	stresses the *i*; atribui = *er*-*tree*-**b⁰⁰i**	
(g)ua	água = **ah**-*ghwar*	*wa*
(q)ua	qual = *kwahl*	*wah*
(g)ue(n)	aguentar = *er*-**ghwe(y)n**ᵍ-*tahr*	*we*
(q)ue(n)	frequente = *frᵉ*-**kwe(y)n**ᵍ-*tᵉ*	*we*

Nasal vowels and diphthongs

Pronounced as if uttering the sound through the nose – an effect similar to that of a "voiced" humming – the Portuguese nasal vowels and diphthongs are signalled by a "til" (˜) over the vowel, by an **m** at the end of a word, or by **m** or **n** before a consonant. Bear in mind that **m** or **n** after a vowel always cause it to become a nasal sound. Contrary to what is the general case in English, **m** and **n** so placed are not pronounced as distinct consonants.

Again, most of these sounds can only be approximated in an English transcription. Throughout this book, nasalisation is indicated by placing n*ᵍ* after the nasal vowel or diphthong. This symbol should not be taken as suggesting that it is to be pronounced as in the English words song, bring, hang, etc.

Nasal vowels

ã, am, an   as *ung* in *lung* – where the *g* is so indistinct as to be virtually silent.   *ahnᵍ*
maçã = *mer*-**sahnᵍ**; campo = **kahnᵍ**-*pᵒᵒ*;
canto = **kahnᵍ**-*tᵒᵒ*

em   também = *tahnᵍ*-**behnᵍ**   *ehnᵍ*

en   cento = **se(y)nᵍ**-*tᵒᵒ*   *e(y)nᵍ*

im, in   as *in* in *sing* – again, standard English usually has the *g* silent   *eenᵍ*
sim = *seenᵍ*; patins = *per*-**teenᵍsh**

12

om, on	as *on* in French *bon*.	*ohn⁹*
	pombo=**pohn⁹**-*b⁰⁰*; conto=**kohn⁹**-*t⁰⁰*	
um, un	chumbo=**shoon⁹**-*b⁰⁰*; fundo=**foon⁹**-*d⁰⁰*	*oon⁹*

Nasal diphthongs

ae, ai	mãe=*mahin⁹*; cãibra=**kahin⁹**-*brer*	*ahin⁹*
ao	(same sound as the final unstressed **am** of verbal forms).	*ah⁰⁰n⁹*
	mão=*mah⁰⁰n⁹*; falam=**fah**-*lah⁰⁰n⁹*	
oe	põe=*pouin⁹*	*ouin⁹*
ui	muito=**mooin⁹**-*t⁰⁰*	*ooin⁹*

Stress

(1) Words ending in -a, -as, -e, -es, -o, -os, -am, -em and -ens are stressed on the last syllable but one (the penultimate syllable).

(2) Most other words, including all those ending in -im, -ins, -um, -uns, -on, -ons, -ã, -ãs, and consonants, are stressed on the last syllable.

Linking of word groups

Whereas in English a momentary pause is normally introduced to avoid the fusion of consecutive words (preventing, for instance, a-nawfu-laccident), in Portuguese the tendency is for an irrepressible liaison of the

13

ending of one word with the beginning of the next, in one same sentence. So it is that:

ele era – e(y)l*e ehrer* – becomes *e(y)*-**leh**-*rer*

nove horas – *nohv*e **hoh**-*rersh* – becomes *noh*-**voh**-*rash*

meus olhos – me(y)°°sh ohll°°sh becomes *me(y)*°°-**zoh**-*ll*°°sh.

Gender

Instead of putting the definite or indefinite article before nouns in the vocabulary lists we have given the gender only. This will enable you to precede the noun with either "a" or "the", depending on the prevailing circumstances. The notes on page 28 will help you further.

A Brief Background to Portugal

Portugal occupies most of the western part of the Iberian peninsula, with the Atlantic Ocean to the west and south and Spain to the east and north. Less than half the size of Great Britain, the country is about 360 miles long and no more than 140 miles wide. The population is just over 9 million. For administrative purposes the country includes the Azores and Madeira—two groups of islands hundreds of miles out in the Atlantic. The main rivers, rising in Spain, are the Tagus (Tejo), Douro and Guadiana, and the principal highlands—in the north and central parts of the country—culminate in the Serra da Estrela behind Coimbra. This range reaches 6,500 feet; far lower are the Serra de Monchique and Serra do Malhão in the deep south. But although the latter mountains are at most 1,900 feet or so high, the protection they afford the Algarve area ensures it a climate which at times smacks of sub-tropical parts. In general Portugal enjoys a milder climate than does Spain; rainfall is greater, and the winters warmer than they are to the east.

Portugal's most famous product is perhaps her port wine (from Oporto, or Porto in Portuguese), but she is also the world's major producer of cork and is well established agriculturally. Sardines, of course, are an important source of revenue. There is little heavy industry, but in recent years the manufacture and export of cotton textiles has assumed a greater importance.

Although Portugal (first known as Lusitania) had her fair share of visits, peaceful and otherwise, from Phoenicians to Moors, her history as an independent country really started in the 11th century. This was when the northern regions between Minho and Douro were given to Henry the Young, a Count of Burgundy, as a dowry on his marriage to a daughter of the King of Leon. At this time the south was controlled by the Moors. In 1147 Afonso I captured Lisbon and established the southern frontier of the country on the banks of the Tagus, but over a hundred years passed before Afonso III finally threw out the Moors and established the frontiers we know today. The first commercial treaty with England was signed in 1294 and an unbroken alliance between the two countries dates from 1373. It was under this same ancient alliance that Portugal leased air bases in the Azores to Britain during the Second World War.

The Portuguese enjoyed their greatest moments of national triumph during the 15th and 16th centuries, when famous explorers such as Prince Henry the Navigator, Bartolomeu Dias and Vasco da Gama sailed the world. They opened up sea routes to India, explored the coasts of Africa, and discovered Brazil. The colonies established in these three areas, and in the East Indies, were extremely wealthy and were ruled by an absolute monarchy which (in 1580) was claimed by Philip II of Spain. For fifty years or so the Portuguese suffered this Spanish dominance, but the crown was restored to the house of Bragança in 1640 and then followed a war of independence that ended in 1668 with the Spanish ousted for good. The alliance with England (strengthened in 1663 by the marriage of Charles II to Catherine of Bragança) was further tested by common action against the French during the Peninsular War in the early 1800s.

Portugal's centuries as a kingdom ended in 1910 when Manoel II was forced to flee the country; two years previously his father and elder brother had been assassinated. A republic was proclaimed, and in 1932 Dr. Salazar became prime minister and virtual dictator until his death in 1970.

A great maritime history has gained for Portugal a hoard of treasure, still to be seen in the many palaces and cathedrals, and masterpieces of art and architecture. Lisbon was razed by an earthquake in 1755 and owes a great debt to the Marquês de Pombal who rebuilt such a beautiful capital city. The pavements of the Rossio (the business centre) are set with striking black and white mosaics; there are lively quays, wide boulevards, magnificent public gardens and a most colourful old quarter at Alfama. Oporto, the northern capital, is famous for its wine and hospitality. The principal vineyards (*quintas*) lie in the picturesque regions of Minho and Trás-os-Montes, to the north and east of Oporto. Traces of the past are to be found all over the country: Roman remains at Évora, Germanic-style buildings in Braga influenced by a 5th century invasion of the north by Frankish tribesmen, Moorish houses in the Algarve, Baroque and Gothic churches, Manueline monasteries and Renaissance buildings abound – in many there are examples of several styles of architecture. In the world of literature Portugal has been influenced by Italian and French authors' styles from an early period. Much inspiration came from the colonial expansion in the 16th century, and the most notable author of this or any other period must be Camões; his epic poem describing Vasco da Gama's journey to India encompasses many other facets of Portuguese history and life. Although this poem, *Os Lusíadas*, took 17 years of his rather unhappy life to write, the inevitable streak of melancholy that pervades it is common to a great deal of Portuguese literature. This trait is more of a typical national quirk than anything else – much in the same way that a great deal of (say) Irish literature is recognisable as such by certain details of style.

17

Social Habits and Customs

The Portuguese are probably the most well-mannered people in Europe and their lives appear to be ruled by many common (and uncommon) courtesies. They are a home-loving race, tending to have large families, and are inclined to keep themselves to themselves. You are less likely to encounter them dining out in a restaurant than you are the inhabitants of other European countries, but the men still use the cafe a great deal as a venue for business discussions and social chit-chat. It is, even now, largely a male-dominated society. You will find the average Portuguese less ebullient than his other Latin neighbours, but just below his apparently serious manner lies a quiet sense of humour.

Although their inherent good manners ensure that a stranger will be accorded every civility and kindness, despite his having made some sort of social blunder, it is only right that you should make an effort to observe the various courtesies and formalities necessary even between friends. For example, when you make a request always add the words "faz favor" (pronounced *fahsh fer-***vour** and meaning "please") in a questioning tone, otherwise you'll be considered rude for giving what appears to be an order. This applies as much to the cafe waitress or lift attendant as it does to your Portuguese friends. Another important phrase, meaning "thank you very much", is "muito obrigado" (**mooin**ᵍ-*t* ᵒᵒ

18

*ou-bri-***ghah***´-d°°*). You will invariably be addressed as "vossa excelencia"; if you know a person's surname, use it preceded by "O Senhor" (*oo s*ᵉ*-***nnour**, Mr.) or "Senhora dona" (*s*ᵉ*-***nnou***-rer* **dou***-ner*, Mrs., followed by her Christian name).

The Portuguese attach great importance to the use of titles, occupational as well as social. As a matter of courtesy, holders of university degrees are addressed as "Senhor doutor", and other (such as business directors and chief engineers) are accorded their qualifications before the fore- and surnames. Although you, as a tourist, may be excused all this seemingly unnecessary formality, it is nonetheless important to know that such niceties exist.

As far as clothing is concerned, men should note that it is customary to wear a suit (or at least a jacket) when dining in the hotel; ladies' trouser suits are accepted everywhere, but only in the big coastal resorts may you wear shorts away from the beach. There is no law against this, but why risk upsetting your hosts by being insensible to their own standards of decency? Bikinis are quite acceptable on all but the more out-of-the-way beaches. When visiting religious buildings, women should keep their heads and arms covered (and – if it can be planned – wear a skirt rather than trousers). Men, too, should roll down their sleeves.

The folklore of Portugal is rich and varied, and zealously preserved in all its traditional purity by folklore groups ("ranchos folclorios" – one wonders why there is not a more Portuguese-sounding word for this!). These groups perform the popular old songs and dances throughout the country; often full of poetry and mystery, these songs and dances vary from region to region and are performed in the local costume. Traditional dress is still worn in some places by people going about their daily tasks; the girls of Nazaré are reputed to wear no less than seven petticoats, while in Apúlia you may see men gathering seaweed for their fields and dressed in unique white linen jackets. The fishermen of Póvoa de Varzim still go to sea in gaily-embroidered shirts, and you will find other places where traditional garb is not simply put on to impress tourists. Folklore "pilgrimages" are very dear to the hearts of the Portuguese, and although they are essentially religious processions and acted out with reverence by the local people, the inevitable conclusion to the day is singing, dancing and fireworks. The nostalgic "fado" – a sad and usually beautiful song of unrequited love, sung to guitars in a candle-lit tavern by black-shawled performers, is as much a part of the Portuguese way of life as is the flamenco to the Spaniard. Lisbon has many "adegas tipicas", or small restaurants that provide fado music as background to your meal.

The Portuguese bullfight differs from the Spanish version in one important aspect – the bull is never killed. Otherwise, it is just as colourful, with splendid pageantry and horsemanship.

Finally, take a look at the following public signs and notices, most of which will directly affect you in one way or another during your stay in Portugal; to know them should help you avoid any embarrassing moments.

PUBLIC NOTICES, ROAD SIGNS

Aberto Open
Água potável Drinking water
Aluga-se For hire, to let
Alugam-se quartos Rooms to let
Autocarros Buses
Banco Bank
Bilheteira Ticket office
Cautela Caution
Cavalheiros Gentlemen
Chamar, chamada Knock, ring
Circulem pela direita/esquerda Keep right/left
Correio(s) Post office
Correspondência Connections
Depósito de bagagem Left-luggage office
Descida íngreme *or* **acentuada** Steep hill
Desvio Diversion
Direcção proibida No entry
Encerrado Closed
Encruzilhada Crossroads
Empurrar Push
É proibido . . . It is forbidden to . . .
É proibida a entrada No entry
É proibido estacionar No parking
É proibido fumar No smoking
Estacionamento proibido No parking
Fechado Closed
Frio Cold
Guiar com cuidado Drive with care
Homens Gentlemen

21

Informação(es) Information
Lavabos Lavatory
Livre Vacant, free, unoccupied
Não pisar a relva Keep off the grass
Não tocar Do not touch
Ocupado Occupied, engaged
Parar Stop
Particular Private
Passagem proibida No overtaking
Passagem de nível Level crossing
Pede-se para não . . . Please do not . . .
Peoes Pedestrians
Perigo Danger
Precaução Caution
Puxar Pull
Reservas Reservations
Retrete(s) Lavatory
Saída Exit
Sala de espera Waiting room
Secção de objectos perdidos Lost property office
Seguir pela direita/esquerda Keep right/left
Senhoras Ladies
Senhores Gentlemen
Sentido proibido No through road
Trabalhos (de estrada) Road works
Trânsito vedado Road closed
Tocar Ring
Velocidade limitada Speed limit

Public Holidays

On the following national holidays, banks, shops and businesses are closed throughout the country:

January 1st (New Year's Day)
Corpus Christi
June 10th (Portuguese National Day)
August 15th (Assumption Day)
October 5th (Republic Day)
November 1st (All Saints' Day)
December 1st (Restoration of Independence)
December 8th (Immaculate Conception)
December 25th (Christmas Day)

Although not official holidays, Shrove Tuesday, Maundy Thursday and Good Friday are – for many shops and businesses – days when they close altogether.

Public Conveniences

These are signed as *Lavabos*, *Retrete* or *Toilette*. The "ladies" is indicated by "*senhoras*", the "gents" by "*homens*", "*senhores*" or "*cavalheiros*". Usually they are quite clean, but more than likely you will come across one of a lower standard – it happens in every country. If unable to find a public lavatory, ask at a cafe, hotel or house:

Please may I use your lavatory?

Dá-me licença que use os lavabos, por favor?

(dah-*m^e lee-***se(y)n**^{g}*-ser k^e* **ooz**^{e} *oosh ler-***vah**-*boosh, poor-**fer**-**vour**?)

23

Useful Everyday Words and Phrases

a, an um, uma *oon^g*, **oo**-*mer*
about cerca de **se(y)r**-*ker d^e*
above em cima de *ehn^g* **see**-*mer d^e*
across através *er-trer*-**vehsh**
after depois *d^e*-**pouish**
again outra vez *ou-trer ve(y)sh*
all todo **tou**-*d^{oo}*
all right está bem *^{e}sh-tah*-**behn^g**
always sempre **se(y)n^g**-*pr^e*
and e *i*
at em *ehn^g*
before antes **ahn^g**-*t^{e}sh*
behind atrás *er*-**trahsh**
below em baixo *ehn^g* **bahi**-*sh^{oo}*
big grande **ghrahn^g**-*d^e*
both ambos **ahn^g**-*b^{oo}sh*
but mas *mersh*
by por *poor*
cold frio **fri**-*^{oo}*
deep profundo *proo*-**foon^g**-*d^{oo}*
dirty sujo **soo**-*zh^{oo}*
down abaixo *er*-**bahi**-*sh^{oo}*
each cada **ker**-*der*
early matutino *mer-too*-**tee**-*n^{oo}*
enough bastante *bersh*-**tahn^g**-*t^e*
everybody todos **tou**-*d^{oo}sh*

everything tudo **too-***d*^{oo}
everywhere em toda a parte *ehn*^g *tou-d' ah* **pahr-***t*^e
far longe **lohn**^g*-zh*^e
fast rápido **rrah-***pi-d*^{oo}
first primeiro *pree-***me(y)i-***r*^{oo}
food comida *koo-mee-**der**
for por, para *poor,* **per-***rer*
from de *d*^e
full cheio **she(y)i-**^{oo}
good bom *bohn*^g
half metade *m*^e*-tah-d*^e
he ele *m.* **e(y)-***le*
here aqui *er-kee*
hers sua *f.,* suas *f.pl.* **soo-***er,* **soo-***ersh*
high alto **ahl-***to*
his seu *m.,* seus *m.pl.* *se(y)*^{oo}, *se(y)*^{oo}*s*
hot quente *ke(y)n*^g*-te*
how? como? *kou-m*^{oo}
how many? quantos? **kwahn**^g*-t*^{oo}*sh*
how much? quanto? **kwahn**^g*-t*^{oo}
I eu *e(y)*^{oo}
in, into dentro *dehn*^g*-tr*^{oo}
it ele *m.,* ela *f.* **e(y)-***le,* *eh-ler*
late tarde *tahr-d*^e
left (*opp. right*) esquerdo ^e*sh-***ke(y)r-***d*^{oo}
less menos **me(y)-***n*^{oo}*sh*
to like gostar de *goosh-***tahr** *d*^e
little pouco *pou-k*^{oo}
lost perdido *p*^e*r-dee-d*^{oo}
many muitos *mooin*^g*-t*^{oo}*sh*
more mais *mahish*

25

much muito **mooin***ᵍ*-*t*ᵒᵒ

my, mine meu *m.*, minha *f.* *me*(*y*)ᵒᵒ, mee-*nner*

near perto **pehr**-*t*ᵒᵒ

new novo **nou**-*v*ᵒᵒ

next próximo **proh**-*si*ᵉᵉ-*m*ᵒᵒ

no, not não **nah**ᵒᵒ*n*ᵍ

of de *d*ᵉ

on em *ehn*ᵍ, em cima de *ehng* **see**-*mer d*ᵉ

open aberto *er*-**behr**-*t*ᵒᵒ

to open abrir *er*-**breer**

or ou *ou*

our nosso *m.*, nossa *f.* **noh**-*s*ᵒᵒ, noh-*ser*

out, outside fora **foh**-*rer*

please por favor, faz favor *poor fer*-**vour**, *fahsh fe*r-**vour**

pretty bonito **boo**-**nee**-*t*ᵒᵒ

quiet tranquilo **trahn**ᵍ-*kwee*-*l*ᵒᵒ

right (*opp. left*) direito *dee*-**re**(*y*)*i*-*t*ᵒᵒ

same mesmo **me**(*y*)**sh**-*m*ᵒᵒ

she ela **eh**-*ler*

slow lento **le**(*y*)**n**ᵍ-*t*ᵒᵒ

some alguns *ahl*-**ghoon**ᵍ**sh**

somebody alguém *ahl*-**ghehn**ᵍ

something algo **ahl**-*gh*ᵒᵒ

soon cedo **se**(*y*)-*d*ᵒᵒ

straight direito *dee*-**re**(*y*)**i**-*too*

thank you (*said by man*) obrigado *ou*-*bri*-**ghah**-*d*ᵒᵒ
         (*said by woman*) obrigada *ou*-*bri*-**ghah**-*der*

their seus *m.*, suas *f.* **se**(*y*)ᵒᵒ**sh** **soo**-*ersh*

there ali *er*-**lee**

they eles *m.*, elas *f.* **e**(*y*)-*l*ᵉ**sh**, eh-*lersh*

thick grosso **ghrou**-*s*ᵒᵒ

thin fino *fee-n^oo*

this este *e(y)sh-t^e*

those aqueles *er-ke(y)-l^esh*

through por, através de *poor, er-trer-***vehsh** *d^e*

too (= *also*) também *tahng-***behn^a**

too many muitos *mooin^a-t^oosh*

too much demasiado *d^e-mer-zee-ah-d^oo*

under debaixo *d^e-***bahi***-sh^oo*

until até *er-***teh**

up a cima *er* **cee-***mer*

very muito *mooin^a-t^oo*

very much muitíssimo *mooing-***tee***-si-m^oo*

we nós *nohsh*

well bem *behn^a*

what? o quê? *oo ke(y)?*

when? quando? **kwahn^a**-*d^oo?*

where? onde? *ohn^a-d^e?*

which? qual? *kwahl?*

who? quem? *kehn^a?*

why? porquê? *poor-***ke(y)***?*

without sem *sehn^a*

wrong equivocado, errado *i-kee-voo-***kah***-doo, i-***rrah***-doo*

yes sim *seen^a*

you* (*s*) o senhor *m.*, a senhora *f.*

      *oo s^e-***nnour***, er s^e-***nnour***-er*

    (*pl*) os senores *m.*, as senhoras *f.*

      *oosh s^e-***nnour***-esh, ersh s^e-***nnour***-ersh*

your seu *m.*, sua *f.* *se(y)^oo, soo-er*

* = the polite form. Use the familiar (tu *too*, *mf.s.*, vos *vohsh*, *mf.pl.*) only when addressing close friends and children.

27

"A", "an", or "one" is translated **um (oonᵍ)** before masculine nouns, and **uma (oo-*mer*)** before feminine nouns. "The" is translated **o** (*oo*) before masculine singular nouns, and **os** (*oosh*) in the plural; before feminine singular nouns it is **a** (*er*), and **as** (*ersh*) in the plural.

Could you direct me to ...?
Pode mostrar-me o caminho para?
poh-*dᵉ* moosh-**trahr**-*mᵉ* oo ker-mee-*nnᵒᵒ* per-*rer*?

Do you speak English?
Fala inglês?
fah-*ler* eenᵍ-**ghle(y)sh**?

Have you a list of excursions?
Tem uma lista de excursões?
tehnᵍ oo-*mer* leesh-*ter* dᵉ ᵉsh-koor-**souinᵍsh**?

Have you anything cheaper?
Tem mais barato?
tehng mahish ber-**rah**-tᵒᵒ?

How are you?
Como está?
kou-*mᵒᵒ* ᵉsh-tah?

How long does it take to ...?
Que tempo leva até ...?
kᵉ te(y)nᵍ-pᵒᵒ leh-*ver* er-teh ...?

How much is it?
Quanto é?
kwahnᵍ-tᵒᵒ eh?

I am English
Sou inglês
sou eenᵍ-**ghle(y)sh**

I am very sorry
Tenho muita pena
te(y)-*nnᵒᵒ* mooinᵍ-*ter* pe(y)-*ner*

I cannot speak Portuguese   Não sei falar português
  *nah°°n⁹ se(y)i fer-**lahr** poor-too-**ghe(y)sh***

I do not wish to speak to   Não quero falar consigo
you
  *nah°°n⁹ keh-roo fer-**lahr** kohn⁹-see-gh°°*

Go away!   Vá-se embora
  vah-sᵉ ehn⁹-**boh-**rer

I do not understand   Não compreendo
  *nahoon⁹ kohng-pri-**e(y)**n⁹-d°°*

I enjoyed myself   Gostei (diverti-me) imenso
immensely
  *goosh-**te(y)**i (dee-vᵉr-**tee-**mᵉ) i-**me(y)**n⁹-s°°*

I have lost my way   Perdi-me (estou perdido)
  *pᵉr-**dee-**mᵉ (ᵉsh-**tou** pᵉr-dee-d°°)*

I have no time   Não tenho tempo
  *nah°°ng te(y)-nn°° **te(y)**n⁹-p°°*

Is this enough?   Chega?
  she(y)-*gher?*

It is very good   É (está) muito bom
  *eh (ᵉsh-**tah**) moo in⁹-too bohn⁹*

Look!   Veja! (Olhe!)
  ve(y)-*zher!* (**oh-***llᵉ!*)

Please write it down   Tome nota (escreva)
  toh-mᵉ noh-**ter** (ᵉsh-**kre(y)-***ver*)

Thank you for your   Obrigado pela sua
hospitality   hospitalidade
  *ou-bri-**ghah-**d°° pᵉ-ler **soo-**er ohsh-pee-ter-lee-**dah-**dᵉ*

29

This is incorrect Isto está errado
  eesh-*t*^{oo} *^{e}sh*-**tah** *i*-**rrah**-*d*^{oo}

Good morning (evening, Bom dia (boa tarde, boa
night) noite)
  bohn^g **dee**-*er* (**bou**-*er* **tahr**-*d*^{e}, **bou**-*er* **noui**-*t*^{e})

Goodbye Adeus
  er-**de(y)**^{oo}**sh**

We are in a hurry Estamos com pressa
  esh-**ter**-*m*^{oo}*sh* *kohn*^{g} **preh**-*ser*

What is that? O que é isso?
  oo k^e *eh* **ee**-*s*^{oo}?

What is the correct time? Que horas são, exactamente?
  k^e oh-**rersh** sahoon^g, *i*-zah-ter-**me(y)**n^g-*t*^{e}?

Where can I get a . . . ? Onde posso obter (arranjar)
  um *m*, uma *f*
  ohn^g-*d*^{e} poh-*s*^{oo} ohb^e-ter (*er*-**rrahn**^{g}-*zhahr*) *oon*^{g}, **oo**-*mer*?

Would you please speak Por favor, fale devagar?
slowly?
  poor fer-**vour**, **fah**-*l*^{e} *d*^{e}-*ver*-**ghahr**?

Your good health À sua saúde
  ah **soo**-*er* ser-**oo**-*d*^{e}

Mr., Mrs., Miss Sr. (senhor), Sra. D.
  (senhora dona), Menina
  s^e-**nnour**, *s*^{e}-**nnou**-*rer* **dou**-*ner*, *m*^{e}-**nee**-*ner*

30

DAYS OF THE WEEK, MONTHS AND SEASONS

Sunday Domingo *doo-**meen**ᵍ-ghᵒᵒ*
Monday Segunda-feira *sᵉ-**ghoon**ᵍ-der-**fe(y)i**-rer*
Tuesday Terça-feira **te(y)r**-*ser*-**fe(y)i**-*rer*
Wednesday Quarta-feira **kwahr**-*ter*-**fe(y)i**-*rer*
Thursday Quinta-feira **keen**ᵍ-*ter*-**fe(y)i**-*rer*
Friday Sexta-feira **saysh**-*ter*-**fe(y)i**-*rer*
Saturday Sábado **sah**-*ber*-*dᵒᵒ*

January Janeiro *zher*-**ne(y)i**-*rᵒᵒ*
February Fevereiro *fᵉ-vᵉ*-**re(y)i**-*rᵒᵒ*
March Março **mahr**-*sᵒᵒ*
April Abril *er*-**breel**
May Maio **mahi**-*ᵒᵒ*
June Junho **joo**-*nnᵒᵒ*
July Julho **joo**-*llᵒᵒ*
August Agosto *er*-**ghoush**-*tᵒᵒ*
September Setembro *sᵉ*-**te(y)n**ᵍ-*br*-*rᵒᵒ*
October Outubro *ou*-**too**-*brᵒᵒ*
November Novembro *noo*-**ve(y)n**ᵍ-*brᵒᵒ*
December Dezembro *de*-**ze(y)n**ᵍ-*brᵒᵒ*

Spring Primavera *pree-mer*-**veh**-*rer*
Summer Verão *vᵉ*-**rah**ᵒᵒ**ng**
Autumn Outono *ou*-**tou**-*nᵒᵒ*
Winter Inverno *een*ᵍ-**vehr**-*nᵒᵒ*

31

NUMBERS

1 Um *m*, uma *f*
  oon^g, **oo**-*mer*
2 Dois *m*, duas *f*
  douish, **doo**-*ersh*
3 Três
  tre(y)sh
4 Quatro
  kwah-*tr^{oo}*
5 Cinco
  seen^g-*k^{oo}*
6 Seis
  se(y)ish
7 Sete
  seh-*t^e*
8 Oito
  oui-*t^{oo}*
9 Nove
  noh-*v^e*
10 Dez
  dehsh
11 Onze
  ohn^g-*z^e*
12 Doze
  dou-*z^e*
13 Treze
  tre(y)-*z^e*
14 Quatorze
  *ka-***tour**-*z^e*

15 Quinze
  keen^g-*z^e*
16 Dezasseis
  *d^e-zer-***se(y)ish**
17 Dezassete
  *d^e-zer-***seh**-*t^e*
18 Dezoito
  *d^e-***zohi**-*t^{oo}*
19 Dezanove
  *d^e-zer-***noh**-*ve*
20 Vinte
  veen^g-*te*
21 Vinte e um *m*, e uma *f*
  veen^g-*ti-oon^g*, *i-***oo**-*mer*
22 Vinte e dois *m*, e duas *f*
  veen^g-*ti-douish*,
  *i-***doo**-*ersh*
23 Vinte e três
  veen^g-*ti-tre(y)sh*
30 Trinta
  treen^g-*ter*
40 Quarenta
  *kwer-***re(y)n^g**-*ter*
50 Cinquenta
  seen^g-*kwe(y)n^g-ter*
60 Sessenta
  *s^e-***se(y)n^g**-*ter*

32

70 Setenta
*s^e-**te(y)n**^g-ter*

80 Oitenta
*oui-**te(y)n**^g-ter*

90 Noventa
*noo-**ve(y)n**^g-ter*

100 Cem (cento)
*sehn^g(**ce(y)ng**-too)*

200 Duzentos
*doo-**ze(y)ng**-toosh*

1000 Mil (um milhar)
meel
*(oon^g mee-**llahr**)*

2000 Dois mil
douish meel

$\frac{1}{4}$ Um quarto
*oon^g **kwahr**-t^{oo}*

$\frac{1}{2}$ Meio (metade)
***me(y)i**-^{oo}*
*(m^e-**tah**-d^e)*

$\frac{3}{4}$ Três quartos
*tre(y)sh **kwahr**-t^{oo}sh*

$\frac{1}{3}$ Um terço
*oon^g **te(y)r**-s^{oo}*

1st Primeiro *m*, -a *f*
*pree-**me(y)i**-r^{oo}, rer*

2nd Segundo *m*, -a *f*
*s^e-**ghoon**^g-d^{oo}, -der*

3rd Terceiro *m*, -a *f*
*t^er-**se(y)i**-r^{oo}, -rer*

TIME

today hoje **ou**-*zh^e*
yesterday ontem **ohn**^g-*tehn^g*
tomorrow amanha *ah-mer-**nnahn**^g*
next year próximo ano **proh**-*see-m^{oo} er-n^{oo}*
last year ano passado **er**-*n^{oo} per-sah-d^{oo}*
this morning esta manhã **ehsh**-*ter mer-**nnahn**^g*
this afternoon esta tarde **ehsh**-*ter **tahr**-d^e*
this evening esta noite **ehsh**-*ter noui-t^e*
last night a noite passada (ontem à noite)
      *er **noui**-t^e per-sah-der (**ohn**^g-tehn^g ah **noui**-t^e)*
tomorrow night amanhã à noite
      *ah-mer-**nnahn**^g ah **noui**-t^e*

33

next week próxima semana, semana que vem
        proh-*see-mer s*ᵉ-**mer**-*ner, se*-**mer**-*ner k*ᵉ *vehn*ᵍ

last week a semana passada *er s*ᵉ-**mer**-*ner per*-**sah**-*der*

minute minuto *mi*-**noo**-*t*ᵒᵒ

hour hora **oh**-*rer*

day dia **dee**-*er*

fortnight quinzena *keen*ᵍ-**ze**(y)-*ner*

month mês *me*(y)*sh*

early cedo **se**(y)-*d*ᵒᵒ

late tarde **tahr**-*d*ᵉ

one o'clock uma hora **oo**-*mer* **oh**-*rer*

quarter past one uma e um quarto
        oo-*mer i oon*ᵍ **kwahr**-*t*ᵒᵒ

13.15 hours treze (horas) e quinze (minutos)
        tre(y)-*z*ᵉ (**oh**-*rersh*) *i* **keen**ᵍ-*z*ᵉ (*mee*-**noo**-*t*ᵒᵒ*sh*)

half past two duas e meia **doo**-*ersh i* **me**(y)i-*er*

14.30 hours quatorze (horas) e trinta (minutos)
        ker-**tour**-*ze i* **treen**ᵍ-*ter*

quarter to two duas menos quinze
        doo-*ersh* **me**(y)-*noosh* **keen**ᵍ-*z*ᵉ

three o'clock três horas *tre*(y)*sh* oh-*rers*

twelve o'clock meio-dia (doze horas)
        me(y)i-ᵒᵒ **dee**-*er* (*dou*-*z*ᵉ **oh**-*rersh*)

noon meio-dia **me**(y)i-ᵒᵒ-**dee**-*er*

midnight meia-noite **me**(y)i-*er*-**noui**-*t*ᵉ

34

COLOURS

black preto (negro) **pre(y)**-*t⁰⁰* (**ne(y)**-*gr⁰⁰*)
white branco **brahn**ᵍ-*k⁰⁰*
red encarnado (vermelho)
    *e(y)n*ᵍ-*ker*-**nah**-*d⁰⁰* (*vᵉr*-**mer**-*ll⁰⁰*)
orange cor de laranja *kour dᵉ ler*-**rahn**-*zher*
yellow amarelo *er-mer*-**reh**-*l⁰⁰*
green verde **ve(y)r**-*dᵉ*
blue azul *er*-**zool**
indigo anil *er*-**neel**
violet violeta *vee-oo*-**le(y)**-*ter*
brown castanho *kersh*-**ter**-*nn⁰⁰*
grey cinzento *seen*ᵍ-**ze(y)n**ᵍ-*t⁰⁰*
beige beige **beh**-*zhᵉ*
pink cor-de-rosa *kour-dᵉ*-**roh**-*zer*
mauve roxo *rrou*-**sh⁰⁰**
purple púrpura (lilás) **poor**-*poo-rer* (*lee*-**lahsh**)
dark escuro *ᵉsh*-**koo**-*r⁰⁰*
light claro **klah**-*r⁰⁰*

Hotels, Accommodation

    Portuguese hotels are now classified according to the usual 5-star system. Previously they were de luxe, 1st A, 1st B, 2nd and 3rd class. Prices are controlled by the State Tourist Department, which publishes a yearly guide to the different types of accommodation. Every hotel must display a price list at its entrance, and in every bedroom; tariffs are either for room only, or for full board consisting of room, breakfast, lunch and dinner. Note that 10% is added to the cost of all meals, other than breakfast, that are served in your room. Children under eight get a 50% reduction on the price of meals. There is a 10% service charge added to all bills, with a further 3·1% charged in tourist resorts.

As well as hotels, there are other categories of accommodation coming under the same control. *Pousadas* are State-owned inns, intended primarily for motorists, in country areas where there are few other establishments in which to spend a night or two. The length of stay in a *pousada* is limited to five days during June–October, and the cost is lower than at other hotels. Privately run, they are often converted buildings of historical interest; most are classified as 4-star, although a few 5-star places exist. *Motels* are less well appointed, being 3- and 2-star. The small hotels known as *estalagens* are very comfortable and are classified as 5- or 4-star, with most rooms having their own bathrooms. Finally, there are numerous *pensões* (*pensions*), ranging from 1-star to 5-star (the latter are also called *albergarias*). Usually run and owned by a family, these boarding houses are comfortably but simply endowed with the essential requirements. It should be noted that in "full board" *pensões* you may be liable to pay up to 20% on the official price quoted for lodging on any occasion that you eat "out".

Electric Current

In Portugal and Madeira this is 220/240 volts A.C. In the Azores it is 110 and 220 volts A.C. Shaving points are in most hotels and you should remember to take a continental two-pin plug as these are thinner and set wider apart than the British version.

USEFUL WORDS AND PHRASES

ashtray cinzeiro *m.* **seen***^{g}***-ze(y)i-r***^{oo}*
basin bacia *f.* *ber-***see***-a*
bath banho **ber-***nn***^{oo}*
bathroom casa de banho *f.* **kah-***zer d^e* **ber-***nn***^{oo}*
bed cama *f.* **ker-***mer*
bedroom quarto *m.* **kwahr-***t***^{oo}*
(double) quarto de casal *m.* **kwahr-***t***^{oo}* *d^e* *ker-***zahl**
bill conta *f.* **kohn***^{g}***-ter**
blanket cobertor *m.* (manta) *f.*
     *k***^{oo}***-b^{e}r-***tour** (**mahn***^{g}***-ter**)
board (full) pensão completa *f.*
     *pe(y)n***^{g}***-sah***^{oo}***n***^{g}* *kohn***^{g}***-pleh-ter*
board (half) meia-pensão *f.* *me(y)i-er pe(y)n***^{g}***-sah***^{oo}***ng*
breakfast pequeno almoço *m.* *p^e-***ke(y)***-n***^{oo}* *ahl-***mou***-s***^{oo}*
chair cadeira *f.* *ker-***de(y)i***-rer*
chambermaid empregada de quarto *f.*
     *e(y)n***^{g}***-pr^e-***ghah***-der d^e* **kwahr-***t***^{oo}*

---

coat-hanger cabide *m. ker-bee-d^e*
dining room sala de jantar *f. sah-ler d^e zhahn^g-tahr*
dinner jantar *m. zhan^g-tahr*
eiderdown (not used in Portugal – in its place, is the
"*colcha*" *f.*, **koul**-*sher*, i.e., the counterpane)
hotel hotel *m. oh-tehl*
hot water bottle botija de água quente
    boo-tee-zher d^e ah-ghwer **ke(y)**n^g-t^e
key chave *f.* **shah**-*v^e*
lavatory retrete *f. r^e-***treh**-*t^e* ("*lavatório*" *ler-ver-toh-ri-^oo*
    is the wash basin)
lift elevador *m. i-l^e-ver-***dour**
light bulb lâmpada *f.* (eléctrica)
    lahn^g-*per-der* (*i-***leh**-*tree-ker*)
manager gerente *m. zh^e-***re(y)**n^g-*t^e*
mattress colchão *m. koul-shah^oo*n^g
message recado *m. r^e-***kah**-*d^oo*
page boy paquete, mandarete
    *per-***ke(y)**-*t^e, mahn-der-***re(y)**-*t^e*
pillow almofada *f.* **ahl**-*moo-***fah**-*der*
porter porteiro *m.* **poor**-*te(y)-r^oo*
proprietor proprietário (dono) *m.*
    *proo-pree-eh-***tah**-*ree-^oo* (**dou**-*n^oo*)
radiator radiador *m. rrer-dee-er-***dour**
reading lamp candieiro *m.*
    kahn^g-*dee-***e(y)**i-*r^oo*
sheet lençol *m. le(y)n^g-***sohl**
shower chuveiro *m. shoo-***ve(y)**i-*r^oo*
soap sabão *m. ser-***bah**^oo*n^g*
switch interruptor *m. een^g-t^e-rroo-p***tour**
table mesa *f.* **me(y)**-*zer*

38

tap (hot, cold) torneira (quente, fria) *f.*
         toor-ne(y)i-*rer* (ke(y)n*ᵍ*-*tᵉ*, free-*er*)
towel toalha *f.* *t°°*-ah-*ller*
wardrobe guarda-vestidos *f.* (guarda-fatos) *m.*
         ghwahr-*der*-*vᵉsh*-tee-*doosh* (**ghwahr**-*der*-fah-*t°°*)
window janela *f.* **zher**-neh-*ler*

I am Mr (Mrs)	Sou . . .
	sou
Have you a room for one night?	Tem um quarto para uma noite só?
	tehnᵍ oonᵍ **kwahr**-*t°°* per-*rer* oo-*mer* **noui**-*tᵉ* soh?
What are your terms?	Quais são as condições? (Qual é o preço?)
	*kwahish sah°°nᵍ ersh kohnᵍ-dee-***souinᵍ**sh? (kwahl eh oo* **pre**(y)-*s°°*)
I wish to stay . . . days (1 week, 2 weeks)	Quero ficar . . . dias (uma semana, duas semanas)
	keh-*r°°* fee-*kahr* . . . **dee**-*ersh* (oo-*mer* sᵉ-*mer*-*ner*, doo-*ersh* sᵉ-*mer*-*nersh*)
May I see the room?	Posso ver o quarto?
	poh-*s°°* ve(*y*)*r* oo **kwahr**-*t°°*
I want a room for myself only	Preciso de um quarto para mim só
	prᵉ-**see**-z°° dᵉ oonᵍ **kwahr**-*t°°* per-*rer* meenᵍ soh
Have you a room with a private bathroom?	Tem um quarto com banho privativo?
	tehnᵍ oonᵍ **kwahr**-*t°°* kohnᵍ ber-*nn°°* pree-ver-**tee**-*v°°*?

Any room will do
Qualquer quarto serve
*kwahl-**kehr** kwahr-t⁰⁰ sehr-vᵉ*

It is too noisy
É muito barulhento
*eh **mooin**ᵍ-t⁰⁰ ber-roo-**lle(y)n**ᵍ-t⁰⁰*

Can I overlook the sea (garden)?
Terei vista sobre o mar (jardim)?
*tᵉ-**re(y)i** veesh-ter sou-brᵉ oo mahr? (zher-**deen**ᵍ?)*

Where is the bathroom?
Onde é a casa-de-banho?
ohnᵍ-di eh er kah-zer dᵉ ber-nn⁰⁰?

May I have a . . . ?
Um m, uma f . . . por favor
*oonᵍ, oo-mer . . . poor fer-**vour***

I only require breakfast
Quero apenas pequeno almoço
*keh-r⁰⁰ er-**pe(y)**-nersh pᵉ-**ke(y)**-n⁰⁰ ahl-**mou**-s⁰⁰*

May I have breakfast in my room?
Posso tomar o pequeno almoço no quarto?
*poh-s⁰⁰ too-**mahr** oo pᵉ-**ke(y)**-n⁰⁰ ahl-**mou**-s⁰⁰ noo **kwahr**-t⁰⁰?*

I require breakfast and an evening meal
Quero pequeno almoço e jantar
*keh-r⁰⁰ pᵉ-**ke(y)**-n⁰⁰ ahl-**mou**-s⁰⁰ i **zhahn**ᵍ-tahr*

I require full board
Quero pensão completa
*keh-r⁰⁰ pe(y)nᵍ-**sah**⁰⁰**nh**ᵍ **kohn**ᵍ-**pleh**-ter*

Does that include all service and taxes?
Estão incluidos o serviço e os impostos?
*esh-**tah**⁰⁰**n**ᵍ een⁰-**kloo**-ee-d⁰⁰sh oo sᵉr-**vee**-s⁰⁰ i oosh een⁰-**pohsh**-t⁰⁰sh?*

What do I do about laundry?	Como posso lavar a roupa?
kou-m°° poh-s°° ler-vahr er rrou-per?	
Can I have a stronger light?	Pode arranjar-me uma luz mais forte?
poh-d^e er-rrahn-zhahr-m^e oo-mer loosh mahish fohr-t^e?	
I am going to bed	Vou deitar-me
vou de(y)i-tahr-m^e	
Please call me at . . .	Por favor, acorde-me à s. . .
poor fer-vour er-kohr-d^e-m^e ahsh . . .	
I shall be back at . . .	Volto às . . .
vohl-t°° ahsh . . .	
Please open (close) the window	Por favor abra (feche) a janela
poor fer-vour ah-brer (fe(y)-sh^e) er zher-neh-ler	
I would like a hot bath	Preciso de tomar um banho quente
pr^e-see-z°° d^e too-mahr oon^g ber-nn°° ke(y)n^g-t^e	
May I have some drinking water?	Arranje-me água para beber, por favor?
er-rrahn^g-zh^e-m^e ah-ghwer per-rer b^e-be(y)r, poor fer-vour?	
I need these clothes washed	Preciso destas roupas lavadas
pr^e-see-zoo dehsh-bersh rou-persh ler-vah-dersh	
Can I have them back tomorrow?	Pode arranjar-mas para amanhã?
poh-d^e er-rrahn^g-zhahr-mersh per-rer ah-mer-nnahn^g?	

41

Would you repair this? Pode consertar isto?
  poh-d^e *kohn*^{g}**-**s^e*r*-**tahr** *eesh*-t^{oo}?

Would you dry these shoes Pode enxugar-me estes
(clothes) for me? sapatos (estas roupas)?
poh-d^e *e(y)n*^{g}**-**sh^{oo}**-ghahr-**m^e *e(y)sh*-t^e*sh* *ser*-**pah-**$toosh$
  (ehsh-$tersh$ **rou-**$persh$)

What time do you close? A que horas fecha?
  er k^e **oh-rersh** **feh-**$sher$?

May I have that table? Posso ocupar esta mesa?
  poh-s^{oo} *oh-koo-***pahr** *ehsh-*ter **me(y)-**zer?

May I dine now? Posso jantar agora?
  poh-s^{oo} *zhahn*^{g}**-tahr** *er-***ghoh-**rer?

May I dine earlier (later) Posso jantar mais cedo
tomorrow? (mais tarde) amanhã?
  poh-s^{oo} *zhahn-***tahr** *mahish* **se(y)-**d^{oo} (*mahish* **tahr-**d^e)
  *ah-mer-***nnahn**^{g}?

May I have the bill? A conta, por favor?
  er **kohn**^{g}*-ter*, *poor fer-***vour**?

Where is my luggage? Onde está a minha
  bagagem?
  ohn^g**-**d^e ^{e}*sh-***tah** *er* *mee-***nner** *ber-ghah-*$zhehn^g$?

Would you get me a taxi? Quer arranjar-me um táxi,
  por favor?
  kehr *er-rrahn*^{g}**-zhahr-**m^e *oon*^{g} *tah-***ksi**^{e}, *poor fer-***vour**?

Thank you for your help Obrigado pela sua ajuda
  ou-bree-gah-d^{oo} p^e*-ler* **soo-**er *er-***zhoo-**der

I have enjoyed my stay Gostei da estadia
  *ghoosh-***te(y)i** *der* ^{e}*sh-ter-***dee-**er

42

Camping and Caravanning

There are at present some sixty camp sites in Portugal, and this number is being added to yearly. Many of the State-run sites have swimming pools, supermarkets, restaurants, playing-fields and other amenities. For the more naturistic camper, many places exist where (with the local authority's permission) one may pitch a tent. All campers should possess a Camping Carnet – either the International Camping Card or a Portuguese "Carta de Campista" (the latter is obtainable from Federação Portugesa de Campismo, Rua da Madalena 75-2, Lisbon).

If you are towing a caravan or trailer, there are two speed limits to watch for: 60 k.p.h., and 40 k.p.h. in built-up areas.

USEFUL WORDS AND PHRASES

bicycle bicicleta *f. bi-see-***kleh**-*ter*
boots botas *f.* **boh**-*tersh*
bridge ponte *f.* **pohn***ᵍ-t*ᵉ
bucket balde *m.* **bahl**-*d*ᵉ
camp acampamento (campismo) *m.*
    *er-kahnᵍ-per-***me(y)n**ᵍ-*t*ᵒᵒ (*kahnᵍ-***peesh**-*m*ᵒᵒ)
to camp acampar *er-kahnᵍ-***pahr**
camping site parque de campismo *m.*
        pahr-*kᵉ dᵉ kahnᵍ-***peesh**-*m*ᵒᵒ

43

canal canal *m.* (*ker*-**nahl**)
cooking utensils apetrechos de cozinha *m.*
　　　　　　er-*p*[e]-**tre(y)-**zee*-*shoosh *d*[e] *k*[oo]-**zee-***nner*
cork screw saca-rolhas *m.* sah-*ker* rou-*ll*.*rsh*
cycle track pista de ciclismo *f.*
　　　　　　peesh-*ter d*[e] *si*-**kleesh-***m*[oo]
cyclist ciclista *si*-**kleesh-***ter*
drinking water água potável
　　　　　　ah-*ghwer poo*-**tah-***vehl*
east este, leste, nascente
　　　　ehsh-*te*, lehsh-*t*[e], *nersh*-**se(y)n***g*-*t*[e]
farm herdade, quinta *f.* ehr-**dah-***d*[e], keen*g*-*ter*
farmer lavrador *m.* ler-*vrer*-**dour**
field campo *m.* kahn*g*-*p*[oo]
forest floresta *f.* floo-**rehsh-***ter*
frying pan frigideira *f.* fr*e*-zhee-**de(y)i***-rer*
groundsheet pano de terra *m.* per-*n*[oo] *d*[e] teh-*rrer*
handlebars guiador *m.* ghee-*er*-**dour**
hike caminhada *f.* ker-mi-**nnah-***der*
hill encosta *f.* e(y)n*g*-**kohsh-***ter*
hitch hike de boleia (ir . . .) *d*[e] boo-**le(y)i***-er* (*eer* . . .)
ice gelo *m.* zhe(y)-*l*[oo]
lake lago *m.* lah-*g*[oo]
log cepo (acha) para queimar, *m.*
　　　　　　se(y)-*poo* (ah-*sher*) per-*rer* ke(y)i-**mahr**
map mapa *m.* mah-*per*
matches fósforos *m.* fohsh-*f*[oo]-*r*[oo]sh
mess-tin marmita *f.* mer-**mee-***ter*
methylated spirits álcool desnaturado *m.*
　　　　　　　　　ahl-**kohl** *d*[e]sh-ner-*too*-**rah-***d*[oo]
mountain montanha (serra) *f.* mohn*g*-ter-*nner* (seh-*rrer*)

mountain pass atalho, caminho *m.*
     er-tah-ll^{oo}, ker-mee-nn^{oo}
north norte *m. nohr-t^e*
paraffin patróleo para queimar *m.*
     p^e-troh-li-^{oo} per-rer ke(y)i-mahr
path caminho *m. ker-mee-nn^{oo}*
penknife canivete *m. ker-nee-veh-t^e*
picnic pique-nique *m. pee-k^e-nee-k^e*
pump bomba *f. bohn^g-ber*
puncture furo *m. foo-r^{oo}*
refuse bin caixote do lixo *m. kahi-shoh-t^e doo lee-sh^{oo}*
repair kit caixa de acessórios ou sobresselentes
     kahi-sher d^e er-se-soh-ree-oosh ou
     soo-br^e-s^e-le(y)n^g-t^esh
river rio *m. rree-^{oo}*
road estrada *f. esh-trah-der*
rope corda *f. kohr-der*
rubbish lixo *m. lee-sh^{oo}*
rucksack muchila *f. moo-shee-ler*
saddle selim *m. s^e-leen^g*
saucepan panela *f. per-neh-ler*
shower (of rain) aguaceiro *m. ah-ghwer-se(y)i-roo*
shower bath banho de chuveiro *m.*
     ber-nn^{oo} d^e shoo-ve(y)i-r^{oo}
sleeping bag saco de dormir *m. sah-k^{oo} d^e doo-meer*
snow neve *f. neh-v^e*
south sul *m. sool*
spoke raio *m. rrahi-^{oo}*
storm tempestade, trovoada *f.*
     te(y)n^g-p^esh-tah-d^e, troo-voo-ah-der
stove fogão *m. foo-ghah^{oo}n^g*

stream riacho, ribeiro *m. ree-ah-sh⁰⁰, ree-be(y)i-r⁰⁰*
summit cume, alto *m.* **koo-***mᵉ*, ahl-*t⁰⁰*
tent barraca, tenda *f. ber-rrah-ker*, te(y)nᵍ-der
tent peg estaca da barraca, *f.*
            *ᵉsh-*tah-*ker der ber-***rrah-***ker*
tent pole vara (mastro) da barraca *f.*
            vah-*rer* (**mahsh-***tr⁰⁰*) *der ber-***rrah-***ker*
thermos termo *m.* **te(y)r-***m⁰⁰*
tin lata *f.* **lah-***ter*
tin opener abre-latas *m. ah-brᵉ-***lah-***tersh*
torch lanterna (lâmpada), *f.*
            *lahnᵍ-***tehr-***ner* (**lahnᵍ-***per-der*)
tyre pneu *m. pne(y)⁰⁰*
valley vale *m.* **vah-***lᵉ*
valve válvula *f.* **vahl-***v⁰⁰-ler*
village aldeia *f. ahl-***de(y)i-***er*
walk passeio *m. per-***se(y)i-***⁰⁰*
to walk andar, caminhar, passear
            *ahnᵍ-***dahr,** *ker-mᵉ-***nnahr,** *per-si-***ahr*
waterfall queda de água *f. keh-***der** *dᵉ ah-***ghwer*
waterproof impermeável *m. een-pᵉr-mi-ah-***vehl*
weather (bad, good) tempo (bom, mau) *m.*
                  te(y)nᵍ-*p⁰⁰* (**bohnᵍ, mah⁰⁰**)
west oeste, poente *m.* *⁰⁰-***ehsh-***te,* *p⁰⁰-***e(y)nᵍ-***tᵉ*
wheel roda *f.* **roh-***der*
wind vento *m.* **ve(y)nᵍ-***t⁰⁰*
wood madeira *f.* (bosque) *m.*
      *mer-***de(y)i-***rer* (**bohsh-***kᵉ*)
youth hostel pousada da juventude *f.*
            *pou-***zah-***der der zh⁰⁰-ve(y)nᵍ-***too-***dᵉ*

46

May I camp here? Posso acampar aqui?
  poh-s^{oo} er-kahn^g-pahr er-kee?

Where is the nearest caravan site? Onde fica o parque de roulottes mais próximo?
  ohn^g-d^e fee-ker oo pahr-ke d^e rroo-loh-tesh mahish proh-si-m^{oo}?

What is the charge per night? Qual é a tarifa por noite?
  kwahl eh er ter-ree-fer poor noui-t^e?

May we light a fire? Pode fazer-se uma fogueira?
  poh-de fer-ze(y)r-s^e oo-mer foo-ghe(y)i-rer?

Where can I buy . . . ? Onde posso comprar?
  ohn^g-d^e poh-s^{oo} kohn^g-prahr . . . ?

Where can I hire a bicycle? Onde posso alugar uma bicicleta?
  ohn^g-d^e poh-s^{oo} er-loo-gahr oo-mer bi-see-kleh-ter?

. . . for a day, a week, two weeks . . . por um dia, uma semana, duas semanas?
  poor oon^g dee-er, oo-mer s^e-mer-ner, doo-ersh s^e-mer-nersh?

May I borrow your . . . ? Pode emprestar-me o seu *m*, a sua *f*
  poh-d^e e(y)n^g-pr^{e}sh-tahr-m^e oo se(y)^{oo}, er soo-er

Motoring

To drive your car in Portugal you must have the familiar "green card", registration book and driving licence – and an International Driving Licence if you enter the country via Spain. If you do not already possess a red warning triangle, you can hire one at the frontier post; they are for setting up whenever you stop on a main road with less than 100 metres' rear visibility – or at night – and should be placed at least 30 metres behind the vehicle.

The rule of the road is: drive on the right, overtake on the left, and give way to traffic coming from the right unless otherwise indicated by the usual international sign. On roundabouts you should give way to vehicles about to enter the circuit. There is a speed limit of 60 k.p.h. in built-up areas unless otherwise indicated, but no limit on the open road. On motorways there is a minimum speed limit of 30 k.p.h. The usual conventional signs are used on all roads, in addition to various pictorial signs denoting sites of interest to the tourist (monuments, beaches, caravan sites and so forth).

Parking: Unless you use a special car park, leave your car on the right-hand side of the road, facing forward – unless a "No Parking" sign is displayed. Some towns have zones where you may park only if you show a parking disc in your window; these discs are obtainable locally. In other places you must park on different sides of the street, on alternate days. Common sense should tell you that parking less than five metres from bends, junctions or hill-tops is not advisable. It is also against the law, as is parking within three metres of a tram stop, or ten metres of a bus stop or where a "No Parking" sign is displayed.

Traffic lights are similar to those in Britain, but there is no amber following the red light; just red for stop, amber for caution and green for go.

Main roads are generally in good repair and are well signposted, but the secondary roads are somewhat rough and "hairy" when right out in the country. Service stations can be hard to find in such areas, and a spare can of petrol is always a worthwhile burden.

USEFUL WORDS AND PHRASES

accelerator acelerador *m. er-s^e-l^e-r-er-***dour**
air pump bomba do ar *f.* **bohn**^*-ber doo ahr*
back axle eixo traseiro (de trás) *m.*
        e(y)i-sh^*oo* trer-**ze(y)i-**r^*oo (de trahsh)*
battery bateria *f.* ber-t^e-**ree-**er
big end capa de biela *f.* **kah-**per de bee-**eh-**ler
body carroçaria *f. ker-rroo-ser-***ree-**er
bolt parafuso de porca *m. per-rer-***foo-**z^*oo de* **pohr-**ker
bonnet capot *m. kah-***pou**
boot mala *f.* **mah-**ler
brake, hand- travão de mão *m. trer-***vah**^*oo*n^*g de* mah^*oo*n^*g*

49

brake lining calces de travão *m.*
            kahl-*s*ᵉ*sh d*ᵉ *trer-vah*ᵒᵒ*n*ᵍ
breakdown avaria, panne *f.* er-ver-**ree**-er, **pah**-*n*ᵉ
breakdown van reboque *m. rr*ᵉ-**boh**-*k*ᵉ
bumper pára-choques *m.* **pah**-rer-shoh-*k*ᵉ*sh*
camshaft vara (tirante) de excêntricos *f. (m.)*
            vah-rer (*tee-rahn*ᵍ-*t*ᵉ) *d*ᵉ *aysh*-**se(y)n**ᵍ-*tree-k*ᵒᵒ*sh*
car carro, automóvel *m.* kah-*rr*ᵒᵒ, *ah*ᵒᵒ-*too-moh*-*vehl*
caravan roulotte *f. rroo*-**loh**-*t*ᵉ
carburettor carburador *m.* ker-boo-rer-**dour**
choke controle do ar *m.* kohn*ᵍ*-**trou**-*l*ᵉ doo ahr
clutch embraiagem *f. ehn*ᵍ-*brahi*-**ah**-*zhehn*ᵍ
distributor distribuidor *m. d*ᵉ*s*-tree-*b*ᵒᵒ*i*-**dour**
door porta *f.* **pohr**-*ter*
to drive conduzir *kohn*ᵍ-doo-**zeer**
dynamo dínamo *m.* **dee**-ner-*m*ᵒᵒ
engine motor *m. m*ᵒᵒ-**tour**
exhaust escape *m.* ᵉ*sh*-**kah**-*p*ᵉ
fan ventoínha *f.* ve(y)n*ᵍ*-too-**ee**-nner
fan belt correia da ventoínha *f.*
            *k*ᵒᵒ-**rre(y)i**-er der ve(y)n*ᵍ*-*t*ᵒᵒ-**ee**-*nner*
funnel funil *m. foo*-**neel**
garage garagem *f. g*her-**rah**-*zhehn*ᵍ
gear marcha, velocidade *f.* **mahr**-*sher*, *v*ᵉ-*loo-see*-**dah**-*d*ᵉ
gear-box caixa de velocidades *f.*
            kahi-*sher d*ᵉ *v*ᵉ-*loo-see*-**dah**-*desh*
gear lever alavanca de velocidades *f.*
            er-ler-**vahn**ᵍ-*ker d*ᵉ *ve-loo-see*-**dah**-*desh*
handle manivela *f.* mer-nee-**veh**-*ler*
hood capota *f. k*er-**poh**-*ter*
horn buzina *f. boo*-**zee**-*ner*

highway code Código de Estrada *m.*
    koh-*dee-gh°°* d*e* *e*sh-**trah**-*der*
hub cap tampão *m.* *tahn*g-**pah**°°n*g*
ignition ignição *m* ee-**ghnee**-**sah**°°n*g*
ignition key chave de ignição *m.*
    shah-*ve* d*e* ee-**ghnee**-**sah**°°n*g*
indicator indicador (pisca-pisca) *m.*
    *een*g-dee-ker-**dour** (peesh-*ker*-peesh-*ker*)
inner tube câmara de ar *f.* ker-*mer-rer* d*e* *ahr*
jack macaco (hidráulico) *m.*
    mer-kah-*k°°* (ee-**drah**°°-lee-*k°°*)
lever manivela *f.* *mer*-nee-veh-*ler*
licence (driving) carta de condução *f.*
    kahr-*ter* d*e* kohn-doo-**sah**°°n*g*
lights (head) (faróis) máximos *m.*
    (*fer*-**rohish**) mah-**see**-m°°sh
lights (side) (faróis) mínimos *m.*
    (*fer*-rohish) mee-nee-m°°sh
lights (rear) luzes de trás *f.* **loo**-*zesh* d*e* *trahsh*
lorry camião *m.* *kah*-mee-ah°°n*g*
lubrication lubrificação *f.* *loo*-bri-fee-ker-**sah**°°n*g*
mechanic mecânico *m.* *m*e-ker-**nee**-k°°
mirror espelho (retrovisor) *m.*
    *e*sh-**pe(y)**-*ll°°* (*rreh*-troh-vee-**zour**)
motorway auto-estrada *f.* *ah*°°-toh-*e*sh-**trah**-*der*
number plate chapa de matrícula *f.*
    shah-*per* d*e* mer-**tree**-k°°-*ler*
nut porca *f.* **pohr**-*ker*
oil óleo *m.* **oh**-*li*-°°
pedestrian peão *m.* pee-**ah**°°n*g*
petrol gasolina *f.* *gher*-z°°-**lee**-*ner*

petrol pump bomba de gasolina *f.*
      bohn^g-*ber d*^{e} *gher-z*^{oo}-**lee**-*ner*

piston ring segmento do pistão *m.*
      *sehgh-***me(y)ng**-*t*^{oo} *doo peesh-***tah**^{oo}**n**^{g}

plug vela *f.* **veh**-*ler*

radiator radiador *m.* *rrer-di-er-***dour**

rim aro *m.* **ah**-*r*^{oo}

screw parafuso *m.* *per-rer-***foo**-*z*^{oo}

screwdriver chave de parafusos *f.*
      shah-*v*^{e} *d*^{e} *per-rer-***foo**-*z*^{oo}*sh*

shock absorber amortecedor *m.* *er-moor-t*^{e}-*s*^{e}-**dour**

to skid patinar *per-tee-***nahr**

spanner chave de porcas *f.* **shah**-*v*^{e} *d*^{e} *pohr-***kersh**

spares sobresselentes *m.* *soo-br*^{e}-*s*^{e}-**le(y)n**^{g}-*tesh*

speed velocidade *f.* *v*^{e}-*loo-see-***dah**-*d*^{e}

speed limit limite de velocidade *m.*
      l^e-**mee**-*t*^{e} *d*^{e} *v*^{e}-*loo-see-***dah**-*d*^{e}

speedometer velocímetro *m.* *v*^{e}-*loo-***see**-*m*^{e}-*tr*^{oo}

spring mola *f.* **moh**-*ler*

starter motor de arranque *m.* *moo-***tour** *d*^{e} *er-***rrahn**^{g}-*k*^{e}

steering wheel volante *m.* *v*^{oo}-**lahn**^{g}-*t*^{e}

tank depósito *m.* *d*^{e}-**poh**-*zi-t*^{oo}

traffic lights luzes de trânsito *f.* **loo**-*zesh d*^{e} **trahn**^{g}-*zee-t*^{oo}

trailer reboque *m.* *rr*^{e}-**boh**-*k*^{e}

transmission transmissão *f.* *trahn*^{g}*sh-mee-***sah**^{oo}**n**^{g}

two-stroke mixture mistura para motor a dois tempos *f.*
      m^e*sh-too-rer* **per**-*rer moo-***tour** *er*
      douish **te(y)n**^{g}-*poosh*

tyre pneu *m.* *pne(y)*^{oo}

tyre (tubeless) pneu (sem câmara de ar) *m.*
      pne(y)^{oo} *(sehn*^{g} *ker-mer-rer d*^{e} *ahr)*

valve válvula *f.* **vahl-***v^{oo}-ler*
vehicle veículo *m.* *ve(y)-ee-***k***^{oo}-l^{oo}*
washer anilha *f.* *er-***nee-***ller*
wheel roda *f.* **rroh-***der*
(rear wheel) roda de trás (traseira) *f.*
       rroh-*der d^e trahsh* (*trer-***ze(y)i-***rer*)
(front wheel) roda da frente (dianteira) *f.*
        rroh-*der der* **fre(y)n***^{g}-t^e* (*dee-ahn^g-***te(y)i-***rer*)
(spare wheel) roda sobresselente *f.*
        rroh-*der soo-br^e-s^e-***le(y)n***^{g}-t^e*
window janela *f.* *zher-***neh-***ler*
(rear window) janela de trás (traseira) *f.*
        *zher-***neh-***ler d^e trahsh* (*trer-***ze(y)i-***rer*)
windscreen pára-brisas *m.* **pah-***rer-bree-***zersh**
windscreen wiper limpa pára-brisas *m.*
        leen*^{g}-per-***pah-***rer-bree-***zersh**
wing (mudguard) guarda-lamas *m.*
        ghwahr-*der* **ler-***mersh*

I want some petrol   Preciso de gasolina
(oil, water)   (óleo, água)
    *pre-***see-***z^{oo} d^e gher-***z^{oo}***-lee-***ner* (**oh-***li-^{oo}*, **ah-***gwer*)
Would you check the oil?   Verifique o óleo, por favor
    *v^e-ri-***fee-***k^e oo* **oh-***li-^{oo}*, *poor fer-***vour**
Would you check the tyre   Verifique os pneus, por
pressure?   favor
    *v^e-ri-***fee-***k^e oosh* **pne(y)***^{oo}sh*, *poor fer-***vour**
Do you do repairs?   Fazem reparações?
    fah-*zehn^g* *rr^e-per-rer-***souin***^{g}sh*?
Can you repair the . . . ?   Pode consertar, reparar?
    poh-*d^e kohn^g-s^{e}r-***tahr**, *rr^e-per-***rahr**?

How long will it take? Que tempo leva?
k^e **te(y)n**^*g*-*p*^*oo* leh-*ver*?

I have run out of petrol Acabou-se-me a gasolina
*er-ker-***bou**-*s*^*e*-*m*^*e* *er gher-z*^*oo*-**lee**-*ner*

The engine is overheating O motor aquece demais
*oo moo-***tour** *er-keh-s*^*e* *d*^*e*-**mahish**

May I park here? Posso estacionar aqui?
poh-s^*oo* ^*e*sh-ter-si-oo-**nahr** *er-***kee**?

Where may I park? Onde posso estacionar?
ohn^*g*-*d*^*e* *poh-s*^*oo* ^*e*sh-ter-si-oo-**nahr**?

How far is it to . . .? Qual é a distância até . . .?
kwahl eh er d^*e*sh-**tahn**^*g*-si-er er-**teh** . . . ?

What time does the garage close? A que horas fecha a garagem?
er k^*e* **oh**-*rersh* **feh**-*sher er gher-***rah**-*zhehng*?

My brakes are slipping (binding) Os travões patinam (gripam)
*oosh trer-***vouin**^*g*sh *per-tee-nah*^*oo*ng (**ghree**-*pah*^*oo*n^*g*)

How far is the next garage? Qual é a distância até à próxima garagem?
kwahl eh er d^*e*sh-**tahn**^*g*-si-er er-**teh** *ah* **proh**-*see-mer gher-***rah**-*zhen*^*g*?

How far is the next filling-station? Qual é a distância até à bomba de gasolina mais próxima?
kwahl eh er d^*e*sh-**tahn**^*g*-si-er er-**teh** *ah* **bohn**^*g*-ber d^*e* gher-z*^*oo*-**lee**-*ner mahish* **proh**-*see-mer*?

May I wash my hands? Posso lavar as mãos?
poh-*s*^*oo* *ler-***vahr** *ersh mah*^*oo*ngsh?

Where is the toilet, please?	Onde é a retrete, por favor?
	ohnᵍ-dᵉ eh er rre-treh-tᵉ, poor fer-vour?
May I use your telephone?	Posso usar o telefone?
	poh-sᵒᵒ oo-zahr oo tᵉ-lᵉ-foh-nᵉ?
I want a new fan belt	Preciso de uma correia para a ventoínha
pre-see-zᵒᵒ dᵉ oo-mer koo-rre(y)i-er per-rer er ve(y)nᵍ-tᵒᵒ-ee-nner	
The clutch is slipping	A embraiagem patina
er ehnᵍ-brahi-ah-zhehnᵍ per-tee-ner	
Is this the road to . . . ?	É esta a estrada para . . . ?
	eh ehsh-ter er ᵉsh-trah-der per-rer . . . ?
Would you wipe the windscreen?	Limpe o pára-brisas, por favor
leenᵍ-ᵉᵉ oo pah-rer-bree-zersh, poor fer-vour	
May I park without lights?	Posso estacionar sem luzes?
poh-sᵒᵒ ᵉsh-ter-si-oo-nahr sehnᵍ loo-zᵉsh?	
I want to hire a car for . . .	Preciso de alugar um carro para . . .
prᵉ-see-zᵒᵒ dᵉ er-loo-ghahr oonᵍ kah-rrᵒᵒ per-rer . . .	
Would you fit a new bulb?	Ponha uma lâmpada nova, por favor
pou-nner oo-mer lahnᵍ-per-der noh-ver, poor fer-vour	
Would you mend this puncture?	Conserte este furo, por favor
kohnᵍ-sehr-tᵉ e(y)sh-tᵉ foo-rᵒᵒ, poor fer-vour	
May I borrow . . . ?	Posso usar . . . ?
	poh-sᵒᵒ oo-zahr?

Public Transport

BY RAIL

The Portuguese railway network is sufficient to cover most tourists' requirements, and fares are reasonably cheap. Children under four years travel free and from four to twelve years they pay half fare. On some trains – the faster expresses – there is a supplementary charge. Both first and second class seats are available; you may well decide that the former is preferable despite the additional cost. It is certainly advisable to reserve all seats in advance. If travelling in a group of ten or more, take advantage of the special group ticket reduction – if you plan to go over 1,500 km by rail then it may be worthwhile buying a "kilometric" ticket. But make sure to do this at least a week before travelling.

BY ROAD

Although there is a good network of coach and bus services throughout the country, the rural routes are often rather crowded – to say nothing of erratic in service. The long-distance coach fares are no cheaper than the 2nd class rail fares. Taxis are plentiful in towns, and their charges clearly advertised. Luggage is charged at 50% of the full fare, and tips are in the region of 10%–15%.

BY AIR

Internal air services, if you need to use them, are maintained by TAP between Lisbon and Oporto, Lisbon and Faro. These flights are daily, return. Madeira is also served.

USEFUL WORDS AND PHRASES

air hostess hospedeira do ar *f.* *ohsh-p^e-de(y)i-rer doo ahr*

airline companhia de aviação (via aérea) *f.*
    kohn^g-per-nnee-er d^e er-vee-er-sah^{oo}n^g
    (vee-er er-eh-ri-er)

airport aeroporto *m.* *er-eh-roh-pour-t^{oo}*

alight sair, descer *ser-eer, d^{e}sh-se(y)r*

berth cama (couchette) *f.* **ker**-*mer (koo-***sheh**-*t^e)*

to board embarcar *ehn^g-ber.r-kahr*

boat barco *m.* *bahr-k^{oo}*

booking office bilheteira *f.* *bi-ll^e-te(y)i-rer*

boot mala *f.* *mah-ler*

bus autocarro *m.* *ah^{oo}-toh-kah-rr^{oo}*

carriage carruagem *f* *ker-rroo-ah-zhehn^g*

case mala *f* *mah-ler*

cloudy enublado, enevoado *i-noo-***blah**-*d^{oo}, i-n^e-v^{oo}-***ah**-*d^{oo}*

coach autocarro *m.* *ah^{oo}-toh-kah-rr^{oo}*

compartment compartimento *m.*
    kohn^g-per.r-tee-me(y)n^g-t^{oo}

conductor condutor (revisor) *m.*
    *kohn^g-doo-***tour** *(rr^e-vee-***zour**)*

connection ligação *f.* *lee-gher-***sah^{oo}n^g**

corridor corredor *m.* *koo-rr^e-***dour**

crew pessoal, tripulação *m., f.*
   p^e-soo-**ahl**, *tree-p^{oo}-ler-***sah^{oo}n^g**
deck convés *m. kohn*-**vehsh**
dining car carruagem restaurante *f.*
   *ker-rroo-***ah***-zhehn^g rr^{e}sh-tah^{oo}-***rahn^g***-*t^e*
draught (wind) corrente de ar *f. koo-***rre***(y)n^g-t^e di ahr*
driver motorista *m.* or *f. moo-too-***reesh***-ter*
embark embarcar *ehn^g-ber.r-***kahr**
enquiry office informações (guichet de . . .) *m.*
   *een^g-foor-mer-***souin^g***sh (ghee-***she***(y) d^e . . .)*
entrance entrada *f. e(y)n^g-***trah***-der*
exit saída *f. ser-***ee***-der*
fare bilhete *m. b^e-***lle***(y)-*t^e*
ferry barco *m.* **bahr**-*k^{oo}*
fog nevoeiro, neblina (*f.*) *n^e-voo-***e***(y)i-r^{oo}, n^e-***blee***-ner*
front frente, dianteira (*f.*) *fre*(y)*n^g-t^e, dee-ahn-***te***(y)i-rer*
fumes gases, vapores (*m.*) **ghah**-*z^{e}sh, ver-***pou***-r^{e}sh*
guard guarda (*m.*) *ghwahr-der*
jet aircraft avião a jacto (*m.*) *er-vee-***ah^{oo}n^g** *er* zhah-*t^{oo}*
to land aterrar *er-t^e-***rrahr**
luggage rack porta-bagagem *m.* **pohr**-*ter-ber-***ghah***-zhehn^g*
luggage van furgoneta de bagagem *f.*
   *foor-g^{oo}-***neh***-ter d^e ber-***ghah***-zhehn^g*
observation lounge salão miradouro *m.*
   *ser-***lah^{oo}n^g** *mee-rer-***dou***-r^{oo}*
passenger passageiro *m. per-ser-***zhe***(y)i-r^{oo}*
pilot piloto *m. pee-***lou***-t^{oo}*
platform plataforma *f. pler-ter-***fohr***-mer*
port porto *m.* **pour**-*t^{oo}*
porter carregador, bagageiro *m.*
   *ka-rr^e-gher-***dour**, *ber-gher-***zhe***(y)i-r^{oo}*

quay cais *m. kahish*

rear de trás, traseira *d^e trahsh, trer-ze(y)i-rer*

river rio *m. ri^{oo}*

roof telhado *m. t^e-llah-d^{oo}*

route rota, direcção *f. rroh-ter, dee-reh-sah^{oo}n^g*

runway pista de descolagem *f.*
      peesh-ter d^e d^esh-k^{oo}-lah-zhehn^g

seat lugar *m. loo-ghahr*

seat belt cinto de segurança *m.*
      seen^g-t^{oo} d^e s^e-ghoo-rahn-ser

seat reservation reserva de lugar *f.*
      rr^e-zehr-ver d^e loo-ghahr

ship navio *m. ner-vee-^{oo}*

sleeper carruagem-cama *f. ker-rroo-ah-zhehn^g-ker-mer*

sleeping berth beliche *m. b^e-lee-sh^e*

station estação *f. ^esh-ter-sah^{oo}n^g*

station master chefe de estação *m.*
      sheh-f^e der ^esh-ter-sah^{oo}ng

steamer barco a vapor (or simply, vapor) *m.*
      bahr-k^{oo} er ver-pour

steward (on ships) criado de bordo, *m.*
      kree-ah-d^{oo} d^e bohr-d^{oo}
      (on planes) comissário *m. koo-mee-sah-ree-^{oo}*

stop paragem (alto) *f. per-rah-zhehn^g (ahl-t^{oo})*

take-off descolagem *f. d^esh-koo-lah-zhehn^g*

terminus terminus, estação terminal *f.*
      tehr-mee-noosh, ^esh-ter-sah^{oo}ng t^er-mee-nahl

ticket collector (in trams) conductor (in trains, ferries,
           etc.) revisor *m.*
      kohn^g-doo-tour, r^e-vee-zour

ticket bilhete *m. b^e-lle(y)-t^e*

(single) simples (ida só) **seen^g-pl^{e}sh** (ee-*der soh*)
(return) de ida-e-volta *d^e*-**ee**-*der*-*i*-**vohl**-*ter*
timetable horário *m. oh*-**rah**-*ree*-^{oo}
train combóio *m. kohn^g*-**bohi**-^{oo}
voyage viagem *f. vee*-*ah*-**zhehn**^{g}
waiting room sala de espera *f.* **sah**-*ler d^e ^{e}sh*-**peh**-*rer*
window janela *f.* **zher**-*neh*-*ler*
wing asa *f.* ah-*zer*

Where is the (coach) station? | Onde é a estação (de autocarros)?
ohn^g-*d^e eh er ^{e}sh*-*ter*-**sah**^{oo}**n**^{g} (*d^e ah^{oo}*-*toh*-**kah**-*rr^{oo}sh*)?

I want a single (return) ticket to ... | Um bilhete de ida só (ida-e-volta) para ... por favor
oon^g b^e-**lle**(**y**)-*t^e d^e* **ee**-*der soh* (*ee*-*der*-*i*-**vohl**-*ter*) **per**-*rer* ... *poor* fer-**vour**

I have a reserved seat | Tenho um lugar reservado
te(**y**)-**nn**^{oo} *oon^g* *loo*-**ghahr** *rr^e*-*z^{e}r*-**vah**-*d^{oo}*

Would you find me a seat? | Arranje-me um lugar, por favor
er-**rrahn**^{g}-*zh^e*-*m^e* *oon^g* *loo*-**ghahr**, *poor* fer-**vour**

I would like a non-smoking compartment | Arranje-me lugar num compartimento se não possa fumar
er-**rrahn**^{g}-*zh^e*-*m^e* *oong* *loo*-**ghahr** *noon^g* *kohn^g*-*per.r*-*tee*-**me**(**y**)**n**^{g}-*t^{oo}* (*s^e* *nah^{oo}n^g* **poh**-*ser foo*-**mahr**)

Could I have a window seat? | Há um lugar à janela?
ah oon^g loo-**ghahr** *ah* **zher**-*neh*-*ler*?

This seat is reserved   Este lugar está reservado
e(y)sh-t*e loo*-ghahr *e*sh-tah *rr*e*-z*e*r*-vah-d*oo*

This seat is taken   Este lugar está ocupado
e(y)sh-t*e loo*-ghahr *e*sh-tah oh-k*oo*-**pah**-d*oo*

Could you find me a berth? Arranje-me uma cama,
por favor
er-**rrahn***g-zh*e*-m*e oo-mer* per-*mer*, *poor fer*-**vour**

May I open (close) the   Dá-me licença que abra
window?   (feche) a janela?
dah-*m*e lee-se(y)n*g*-ser k*e* **ah**-brer (**feh**-*she*) er zher-**neh**-ler?

How long do we stop here? Por quanto tempo paramos
aqui?
poor **kwahn***g-t*oo te(y)n*g-p*oo per-rer*-m*oo*sh er-**kee**?

Where is the inspector?   Onde está o inspector
(revisor)?
ohn*g-d*e e*sh-tah oo een*g*sh-peh-**tour** (r*e*-vee-**zour**)?

Please mind my seat   Tome conta do meu lugar,
por favor
toh-*m*e* kohn***g-ter-doo me(y)*oo loo*-ghahr, *poor fer*-**vour**

Where is the dining car?   Onde é o restaurante?
ohn*g-d*e eh oo rr*e*sh-tah*oo*-**rahn***g-t*e?

What time is lunch   A que horas é o almoço
(dinner)?   (jantar)?
*er k*e **oh**-*rersh eh oo* ahl-**mou**-s*oo* (**zhahn***g-**tahr**)?

What time do you leave   A que horas parte (chega)?
(arrive)?
*er k*e **oh**-*rersh* **pahr**-*t*e (she(y)-**gher**)?

I want to get off at ...	Quero sair, (descer) em ...
*keh-r°° ser-**eer**, (d^esh-se(y)r) ehn^g ...*	

I want to get off at ...   Quero sair, (descer) em ...
  keh-r°° ser-eer, (d^esh-se(y)r) ehn^g ...

Will you tell me when we arrive?   Avise-me quando chegarmos, por favor
  er-vee-z^e-m^e kwahn^g-d°° sh^e-ghahr-m°°sh, poor fer-vour

Do you pass ... ?   Passa por ... ?
  pah-ser poor ... ?

How long is the voyage?   Quanto tempo leva a viagem?
  kwahn^g-t°° te(y)n^g-p°° leh-ver er vee-ah-zhehn^g ?

Do you go near ... ?   Passamos próximo de?
  per-ser-m°°sh proh-see-m°° d^e ?

Will you put this (in the boot) (on the roof)?   Pode pôr isto (na mala) (no topo)?
  poh-d^e pour eesh-t°° (ner mah-ler) (n°° tou-p°°)

There is a draught   Faz corrente de ar
  fahsh c°°-rre(y)n^g-t^e di-ahr

Would you please open the window?   Abra a janela, por favor
  ah-brer er zher-neh-ler

May I put this on the rack?   Posso pôr isto no porta-bagagem?
  poh-s°° pour eesh-t°° n°° pohr-ter-ber-ghah-zhehn^g ?

Do you return here?   Volta aqui (regressa aqui)?
  vohl-ter er-kee (r^e-ghreh-ser er-kee) ?

Do you start from here?   É daqui que parte?
  eh der-kee k^e pahr-t^e ?

Porter, can you take this luggage to the left-luggage office?

Carregador, leve-me estas malas para o Depósito de Bagagens, por favor

*ker-rr^e-gher-dour, leh-v^e-m^e ehsh-tersh mah-lersh per-rer oo d^e-**poh**-see-t^{oo} d^e ber-ghah-zhehngsh, poor fer-**vour***

I shall collect it at/on . . .

Irei buscá-las às . . . no dia . . .

*ee-**re**(y)i boosh-kah-lersh ahsh . . . n^{oo} dee-er . . .*

Would you get me a taxi to . . . ?

Arranje-me um táxi para . . . por favor

*er-**rrahn**^{g}-zh^e-m^e oong tah-ksi per-rer poor fer-**vour***

Where is the booking office?

Onde é a bilheteira?

*ohn^g-d^e eh er b^e-lle-**te**(y)i-rer?*

Where is the enquiry office?

Onde são as Informações?

*ohn^g-de sah^{oo}n^g ersh een^g-foor-mer-**souin**^{g}sh?*

What time does the train leave for . . . ?

A que horas parte o combóio para?

*er k^e **oh**-rersh pahr-t^e oo kohn^g-bohi-^{oo} per-rer?*

Which platform, please?

Em que plataforma, por favor?

*ehn^g k^e pler-ter-**fohr**-mer, poor fer-**vour**?*

Is this the right train for . . . ?

É este o combóio para . . . ?

eh e(y)sh-t^e oo kohn^g-bohi-^{oo} per-rer . . . ?

Does it go direct?

É directo?

*eh dee-**reh**-t^{oo}?*

Must I change?   Devo mudar (Tenho
de . . .)?
de(y)-v°° moo-dahr (ter-nn°° d^e moo-dahr)?

Where do I change?   Onde tenho de mudar?
ohn^g-d^e ter-nn°° d^e moo-dahr?

What time is the last train   A que horas parte o
for . . . ?   último combóio para . . . ?
er k^e oh-rersh pahr-t^e oo ool-tee-m°° kohn^g-bohi-°°
           peɪ-rer . . . ?

Where is the nearest   Onde fica o hotel mais
hotel?   próximo?
ohn^g-de fee-ker oo oh-tehl mahish proh-see-m°°?

When can I get a plane   Quando há avião para?
for . . . ?
kwahn^g-d°° ah er-vee-ah°°n^g per-rer?

What time does it leave?   A que horas parte?
     er ke oh-rerks pahr-t^e?

What times does it arrive?   A que horas chega?
     er ke oh-rersh she(y)-gher?

Where does it touch down?   Onde é que aterra?
     ohn^g-d^e eh k^e er-teh-rrer?

Will you fasten (unfasten)   Aperte-me (desaperte-me)
my safety belt?   o cinto de segurança,
     por favor
er-pehr-t^e-m^e (d^e-zer-pehr-t^e-m^e) oo seen^g-t°° d^e s^e-ghoo-
         rahn^g-ser, poor fer-vour?

Have you a map of the   Tem um mapa com a rota,
route?   por favor?
tehn^g oom mah-per kohn^g er rroh-ter, poor fer-vour?

Will you raise (lower) my seat?   Levante-me o assento, (abaixe-me) por favor

*le-***vahn**^g*-t^e-m^e oo er-***se**(y)n^g-t^{oo}, (er-***bahi**-sh^e-m^e)
poor fer-***vour***

What is the weather report?   Como vai estar o tempo?

kou-*m^{oo} vahi ^esh*-**tahr** *oo* **te**(y)n^g-*p^{oo}* ?

May I have some cigarettes?   Posso comprar cigarros?

poh-*s^{oo} kohn^g*-**prahr** *see*-**ghah**-*rr^{oo}sh* ?

Are we on time?   Estamos a tempo?

^esh-**ter**-*moosh er* **te**(y)n^g-*p^{oo}* ?

Would you adjust the air conditioner?   Regule o ar condicionado, por favor

r^e-**ghoo**-*l^e oo ahr kohn^g-dee-see-oo-***nah**-*d^{oo}, poor fer*-**vour**

It is very warm   Está muito quente (está calor)

^esh-**tah** *mooin^g-t^{oo}* **ke**(y)n^g-*t^e* (*^esh*-**tah** *ker*-**lour**)

I do not feel well   Não me sinto bem

nah^{oo}ng m^e **seen**^g-*t^{oo}* **behn**^g

Food and Wine

The general standard of cooking in Portugal is very good, although not in the French class. If you are not fond of olives, then be prepared to put up with them in a variety of dishes – and their oil in cooking generally. You might find it difficult to get food cooked in any other fat.

Soups are outstanding, and include *gaspacho* (a thick mixed soup which varies from region to region), *canja* made from chicken and rice, and *caldo verde* – which is potato, cabbage and (sometimes) sausage meat.

As might be expected, the fish dishes are unsurpassed. Among these is *bacalhau*, for which there are some 350 different recipes! The basic ingredient is dried cod, which may sound off-putting and certainly is no indication of the subtleties found in this succulent dish. From Setúbal come grilled *salmonetes*, (red mullet), and mussels are very popular. Minced crab served with cheese is delicious; called *carro*, it is a speciality of Viano do Castelo. *Sardinha assada*, large grilled sardines, are both appetising and cheap. *Lagosta suada à moda de Peniche*, a lobster cooked in wine with butter, onions and peppers, is another excellent dish. A speciality of northern Portugal – as the name implies – is *lampreia à moda do Minho*, lampreys stewed in red wine and brandy. Large crayfish (*lagostà*) are prepared in a number of ways, most of them expensively.

Meat dishes are less varied, but there are some very tasty regional recipes. *Cozido à portuguesa* is a delightful mixture of beef, salt pork, vegetables and sausage, with rice being added in the north; *sarapatel* – a lamb and kid stew; *porco à Alentejana* – fried chopped pork with olives and clams; and stuffed lamb *à la Braganza*. In southern Portugal you may find that meat dishes in general are not of the highest standard.

Unless you have a particularly sweet tooth, miss the Portuguese desserts. The more popular are *queijadas*, *pão de ló* and *ovos moles* with sugar and almonds. But don't miss the cream cheeses, *Serra* and *Azeitão*, made from goats' and ewes' milk and so soft that you have to use your spoon.

Portugal offers a great variety of palatable table wines, a wide range of ports and brandies, and all are comparatively inexpensive. Local beers (*cerveja*) are not too bad for the price, and there are all the usual soft drinks and colas. Probably the best of the wines are the *vinhos verdes*, very light and slightly sparkling, from the north of the country. Some very good red wines come from Dão and among the many excellent rosés is *Trás os Montes*. The Portuguese drink a dry white port as an aperitif, or a dry Madeira (*Sercial*). A sweet Madeira (*Malvasia*) is excellent for dessert. Two other groups of table wines that are very popular are *Bucelas* – white and rather dry, and *Colares* – red wines from Sintra. Naturally enough, in a country that is economically so dependent on producing its own wines, all imported labels are very expensive.

Restaurants and cafes

It is important to remember – particularly if travelling by car – that you will not encounter so many restaurants once free of the major cities and tourist resorts as elsewhere in Europe. This is because most Portuguese prefer to eat at home. However, most hotels serve meals to non-residents. The food is generally good and ample; prices are still quite moderate when compared with other continental menus.

Breakfast is usually light – rolls, bread or toast with butter and jam, and coffee. Lunch, which is served from noon until about 2.30, will usually consist of soup, hors d'oeuvres, fish or meat with vegetables, a rich sweet, fruit or cheese. Often, people will have a snack at around 5 p.m. Dinner is much the same, and is served from about 7 p.m. The price of a table d'hote meal always includes a small carafe of the local wine, unless you want something more expensive.

USEFUL WORDS FOR THE RESTAURANT
bar bar *m. bahr*
bill conta *f.* **kohn***ᵍ-ter*
bottle garrafa *f. gher-***rrah-***fer*
cup chávena *f. shah-vᵉ-ner*
drink (alcoholic) bebida (alcoólica) *f.*
         *bᵉ-***bee-***der (ahl-kᵒᵒ-oh-lee-ker)*
fork garfo *m.* **ghahr-***fᵒᵒ*
glass copo *m.* **koh-***pᵒᵒ*
knife faca *f.* **fah-***ker*
menu ementa, menu *f., m. i-me(y)nᵍ-ter, mᵉ-***noo**
napkin guardanapo *m. ghwer.r-der-***nah-***pᵒᵒ*

plate prato *m.* **prah-***t^{oo}*
spoon colher *f.* *k^{oo}*-**llehr**
table mesa *f.* **me(y)-***zer*
tip gorgeta *f.* *gh^{oo}r*-**zhe(y)-***ter*
waiter empregado de mesa *m.*
      ehn^{g}-pr^{e}-**ghah-***d^{oo} d^{e}* **me(y)-***zer*
waitress empregada de mesa *f.*
      ehn^{g}-pr^{e}-**ghah-***der d^{e}* **me(y)-***zer*
wine list carta de vinhos *f.* **kahr-***ter d^{e}* **vee-***nnoosh*
FOOD Comida *f.* *k^{oo}*-**mee-***der*
apple maçã *f.* **mer-***sahn^{g}*
banana banana *f.* **ber-***ner-ner*
beans feijão *m.* *fe(y)i*-**zhah***^{oo}n^{g}*
beef carne de vaca *f.* **kahr-***n^{e} d^{e}* **vah-***ker*
biscuit biscoito *m.* *b^{e}sh*-**koui-***t^{oo}*
bread pão *m.* *pah^{oo}n^{g}*
butter manteiga *f.* **mahn^{g}-te(y)i-***gher*
cabbage hortaliça, couve *f.* **ohr-ter-lee-***ser*, **kou-***v^{e}*
cake bolo *m.* **bou-***l^{oo}*
carrots cenouras *f.* *s^{e}*-**nou-***rersh*
cauliflower couve-flor *f.* **kou-***ve-flour*
cheese queijo *m.* **ke(y)i-***zh^{oo}*
chops costoletas *f.* *k^{oo}sh-t*-**le(y)-***tersh*
cream creme *m.*, natas *f.* **kreh-***m^{e}*, **nah-***tersh*
egg ovo *m.* **ou-***v^{oo}*
fish peixe *m.* **pe(y)i-***sh^{e}*
fruit fruta *f.* **froo-***ter*
grapes uvas *f.* **oo-***versh*
ham fiambre *m.* **fee-ahn^{g}-***br^{e}*
ice-cream gelado *m.* *zh^{e}*-**lah-***d^{oo}*
jam compota *f.* **kohn^{g}-poh-***ter*

lamb borrego, cordeiro *m.* *b^oo-rre(y)-gh^oo*, *k^oor-de(y)i-r^oo*
lemon limão *m.* *lee-mah^oon^g*
lobster lagosta *f.* *ler-ghoush-ter*
marmalade compota de laranja *f.*
        kohn^g-poh-ter d^e ler-rahn-zher
melon melão *m.* *m^e-lah^oong*
mushrooms cogumelos *m.* *k^oo-gh^oo-meh-loosh*
mussels mexilhão *m.* *m^e-sh^e-llah^oon^g*
mustard mostarda *f.* *moosh-tahr-der*
oil azeite *m.* *er-ze(y)i-t^e*
onions cebolas *f.* *s^e-bou-lersh*
orange laranja *f.* *ler-rahn^g-zher*
oysters ostras *f.* *oush-trersh*
parsley salsa *f.* *sahl-ser*
peach pêssego *m.* *pe(y)-s^e-g^oo*
pear pera *f.* *pe(y)-rer*
peas ervilhas *f.* *ir-vee-llersh*
pepper pimenta *f.* *pee-me(y)n^g-ter*
pork porco *m.* *pour-k^oo*
potatoes batatas *f.* *ber-tah-tersh*
poultry aves *f.* *ah-v^esh*
rice arroz *m.* *er-rroush*
roll pãozinho, carcaça *m.* *pah^oon^g-zee-nn^oo*, *ker-kah-ser*
salad salada *f.* *ser-lah-der*
salt sal *m.* *sahl*
sauce molho *m.* *mou-ll^oo*
shrimps camarões *m.* *ker-mer-rouingsh*
soup sopa *f.* *sou-per*
sugar açucar *m.* *er-soo-ker.r*
toast torrada *f.* *too-rrah-der*
tomatoes tomates *m.* *t^oo-mah-t^esh*

vanilla baunilha *f. bah⁰⁰-nee-ller*
veal vitela *f. vee-teh-ler*
vegetables legumes *m. lᵉ-ghoo-mᵉsh*
vinegar vinagre *m. vee-nah-ghrᵉ*

DRINKS Bebidas *f. bᵉ-bee-dersh*
aperitif aperitivo *m. er-pᵉ-ri-tee-v⁰⁰*
beer cerveja *f. sᵉr-ve(y)i-zher*
brandy conhaque *m. koh-nnah-kᵉ*
chocolate chocolate *m. sh⁰⁰-koo-lah-tᵉ*
coffee café *m. ker-feh*
gin gin *m. zheenᵍ*
ice gelo *m. zhe(y)-l⁰⁰*
lemonade (fizzy) limonada (gazeificada) *f.*
  lee-moo-nah-der (gher-zᵉ-fee-kah-der)
lemon squash limonada natural *f.*
  lee-moo-nah-der ner-too-rahl
liqueur licor *m. lee-kour*
milk leite *m. lay-tᵉ*
mineral water água mineral *f. ah-ghwer mee-nᵉ-rahl*
orangeade (fizzy) laranjada (gaseificada) *f.*
  ler-rahnᵍ-zhah-der (gher-zᵉ-fee-kah-der)
orange squash laranjada natural *f.*
  ler-rahnᵍ-zhah-der ner-too-rahl
port vinho do Porto *m. vee-nn⁰⁰ doo pour-t⁰⁰*
rum rum *m. rroonᵍ*
soda water soda *f. soh-der*
tea chá *m. shah*
water água *f. ah-ghwer*
whisky whisky *m. weesh-kᵉ*
wine vinho *m. vee-nn⁰⁰*

USEFUL PHRASES FOR THE RESTAURANT

May I (we) have a table? Pode arranjar-me
(arranjar-nos) uma mesa?
poh-d^e **er-rrahn-zhahr-**m^e (*er-rrahn-zhahr-*$n^{oo}sh$) **oo-mer**
me(y)-zer?

May I (we) have a snack? Posso (podemos) tomar
uma refeição leve?
poh-s^{oo} (*poo-***de(y)-**$m^{oo}sh$) *too-***mahr oo-**mer rr^e-fe(y)i-
sah$^{oo}n^g$ leh-*ve*?

We are in a hurry Estamos com pressa
^{e}sh-**ter-**$m^{oo}sh$ kohn^g **preh-**ser

May I have the menu? A ementa, por favor
er i-**me(y)ng-**ter, *poor* fer-**vour**

I do not like highly Não gosto de comida muito
seasoned food apurada (temperada)
nah^{oo}ng ghohsh-t^{oo} d^e k^{oo}-**mee-**der mooing-t^{oo} er-p^{oo}-**rah-**der
(*te(y)ng-p^e-***rah-**der)

I like it well done Gosto de comida bem
passada
ghohsh-t^{oo} d^e k^{oo}-**mee-**der behn^g per-**sah-**der

Medium, under done Meio-termo, mal passada
me(y)i-^{oo}-**te(y)r-**m^{oo}, *mahl* per-**sah-**der

May I have some bread? Arranje-me pão, por favor
er-**rrahn^g-**zh^e-m^e pah$^{oo}n^g$, *poor* fer-**vour**

I will have the set lunch Quero o almoço (jantar)
(dinner) completo
keh-r^{oo} *oo* ahl-**mou-**s^{oo} (*zhahn^g-*tahr) kohn^g-**pleh-**t^{oo}

A little more	Um pouco mais, por favor
oong **pou**-*k^{oo} mahish, poor fer-***vour**	

A little more   Um pouco mais, por favor
oong **pou**-*k^{oo} mahish, poor fer-***vour**

That is enough   Chega, obrigado
*she(y)-gher, ou-bree-***ghar**-*d^{oo}*

May I have the wine list?   Traga-me a carta dos
vinhos, por favor
*trah-***gher**-*m^e* er **kahr**-*ter doosh* **vee**-*nn^{oo}sh, poor fer-***vour**

May I have a (½) flask of   Arranje-me uma (meia)
local wine?   garrafa de vinho da região?
*er-***rrahn**^{g}-*zh^e-m^e* **oo**-*mer* **(me(y)i**-*er)* **gher-rrah**-*fer* *d^e*
vee-*nn^{oo} der* **rr**^e-*zhee-***ah**^{oo}*n?*

Red, white, rosé wine   Vinho tinto, branco, rosé
vee-*nn^{oo}* **teen**^{g}-*t^{oo}*, **brahn**^{g}-*k^{oo}*, *rroo*-**zeh**

I like dry (sweet) wine   Gosto de vinho sêco (doce)
ghosh-*t^{oo} d^e* **vee**-*nn^{oo}* **se(y)**-*k^{oo}* (**dou**-*s^e*)

May I have some water?   Água, por favor
ah-*ghwer, poor fer-***vour**

May I have some coffee?   Café, por favor
ker-*feh, poor fer-***vour**

I do not like fat   Não gosto de gordura
nah^{oo}n^{g} **ghosh**-*t^{oo} d^e* **ghoor-doo**-*rer*

What do you recommend?   Que nos aconselha?
*k^e noosh er-***kohn**^{g}-*se(y)-***ller?**

Would you bring me an   Arranje-me um cinzeiro,
ash-tray?   por favor
*er-***rrahn**^{g}-*zh^e-m^e oon^{g} seen^{g}-***ze(y)i**-*r^{oo}, poor fer-***vour**

I will come back   Eu vou voltar
*eh^{oo} vou vohl-***tahr**

May I reserve a table for . . . ?	Posso reservar uma mesa para . . . ?
poh-*s^{oo}* **rr***^e-z^er***-vahr oo-***mer* **me(y)-***zer* **per-***rer* **. . . ?**	
May I have the bill?	Quer dar-me a conta, por favor?
kehr **dahr-***m^e* *er* **kohn***^g-ter, poor* **fer-vour***?*	
The meal was excellent	A refeição estava óptima
er **rre-fe(y)i-sah***^{oo}***n***^g* *^esh-***tah-***ver* **oh-***tee-mer*	

Shopping

Business hours in general are from 9 a.m. to 1 p.m. and from 3 p.m. to 7 p.m. Mondays to Saturdays – but banks are an exception (see page 94). In the holiday season some shops will stay open later, more especially in tourist resorts.

Of course there is the usual choice of souvenir bric-a-brac to be had, but some may prefer more real reminders of their Portuguese holiday – brilliantly coloured rugs and blankets from Arraiolos (Alentejo), or some similar practical object. Very popular are the attractive baskets from Obidos, the exquisite Peniche lace and all sorts of things made from cork. Portuguese dolls are always in demand, and of these the most exotic are those from the overseas provinces. Gold and silver filigree work is very fine, and the best shopping centre in Lisbon for such articles – and antiques – is the Chiado.

There is an annual trade fair at Belém in April, which shows not only what the Portuguese make in their respective provinces (both home and overseas) but also what they do. It is a very good display of the finest arts and crafts of the entire country.

USEFUL WORDS AND PHRASES

ball point esferográfica *f.* *ᵉsh-feh-roh*-**ghrah**-*fee-ker*

belt cinto *m.* **seen***ᵍ*-*tᵒᵒ*

blouse blusa *f.* **bloo**-*zer*

book livro *m.* **lee**-*vrᵒᵒ*

bracelet pulseira *f.* *pool*-**se(y)i**-*rer*

braces suspensórios *m.* *soosh-pe(y)n*ᵍ-**soh**-*ri*-*ᵒᵒsh*

brassière soutien *m.* *soo-tee*-**ahn***ᵍ*

brooch broche, alfinete *m.* **broh**-*shᵉ*, *ahl-fee*-**ne(y)**-*tᵉ*

buttons botões *m.* *boo*-**touingsh**

cap boné *m.* *boh*-**neh**

cigars charutos *m.* *sher*-**roo**-*tᵒᵒsh*

cigarettes cigarros *m.* *see*-**ghah**-*rrᵒᵒsh*

coat casaco comprido (sobretudo) *m.*
    ker-**zah**-*kᵒᵒ* **kohn**ᵍ-**pree**-*dᵒᵒ* (*sᵒᵒ*-*brᵉ*-**too**-*dᵒᵒ*)

dictionary dicionário *m.* *di-see-oo-nah*-**ri**-*ᵒᵒ*

doll boneca *f.* *boo*-**neh**-*ker*

dress vestido *m.* *vᵉsh*-**tee**-*dᵒᵒ*

ear rings brincos *m.* **breen**ᵍ-*kᵒᵒsh*

elastic elástico *m.* *i*-**lahsh**-*tee*-*kᵒᵒ*

envelope envelope *m.* *e(y)n*ᵍ-*vᵉ*-**loh**-*pᵉ*

girdle cinta *f.* **seen**ᵍ-*ter*

gloves luvas *f.* **loo**-*versh*

gramophone record disco *m.* **deesh**-*kᵒᵒ*

guide book guia (manual) *m.* **ghee**-*er* (*mer-nᵒᵒ*-**ahl**)

handbag mala de mão *f.* *mah-ler d^e mah^{oo}n^g*

handkerchiefs lenços (de assoar) *m.*
 le(y)n^g-s^{oo}sh (d^e er-s^{oo}-ahr)

hat chapéu *m.* *sher-peh^{oo}*

ink tinta *f.* *teen^g-ter*

jacket casaco *m.* *ker-zah-k^{oo}*

jumper camisola de malha *f ker-mee-zoh-ler d^e mah-ller*

lace renda *f.* *re(y)n^g-der*

lighter isqueiro *m.* *eesh-ke(y)i-r^{oo}*
 flint, fuel, gas pedra, gasolina, gás
 peh-drer gher-s^{oo}, ghahsh

map mapa *m.* **mah**-*per*

matches fósforos *m.* *fohsh-f^{oo}-r^{oo}sh*

necklace fio (de pescoço) *m.* **fi**-^{oo} *(d^e p^{e}sh-kou-s^{oo})*

needle agulha *f.* *er-ghoo-ller*

newspaper jornal *m.* *zhoor-***nahl**

nightdress camisa de dormir *f.* *ker-mee-zer d^e door-***meer**

nylons nylons (meias de nylon) *m.*
 *nahi-lohngsh (***me(y)***i-ersh d^e nahi-lohn^g)*

pants (knickers) cuecas *f.* *kw*e-*kersh*

pen caneta *f.* *ker-***ne(y)**-*ter*

pencil lápis *m.* *lah-p^{e}sh*

petticoat saiote *m.* *sahi-oh-t^e*

pipe cachimbo *m.* *ker-sheen^g-b^{oo}*

pin alfinete *m.* *ahl-fee-***ne(y)**-*te*

purse bolsa *f.* *boul-ser*

pyjamas pijama *m.* *p^e-***zher**-*mer*

ring anel *m.* *er-***nehl**

sandals sandálias *f.* *sahn^g-dah-li-ersh*

scarf lenço (da cabeça, do pescoço) *m.*
 *le(y)n^g-s^{oo} (der ker-***be(y)***-ser, doo pesh-***kou**-*s^{oo})*

scissors tesoura *f. t^e-zou-rer*
shawl xaile *m. shahi-l^e*
shirt camisa *f. ker-mee-zer*
shoes sapatos *m. ser-pah-t^oo sh*
shoe laces atacadores *m. er-ter-ker-dou-r^e sh*
shoe polish pomada *f. poo-mah-der*
silk seda *f. se(y)-der*
skirt saia *f. sahi-er*
slip combinação *f. kohn^g-bee-ner-sah^oo ng*
slippers pantufas *f. pahn^g-too-fersh*
soap sabão *m. ser-bah^oo n^g*
socks peúgas *f. pi-oo-ghersh*
spectacles óculos *m. oh-k^oo-loosh*
stockings meias altas *f. me(y)i-ersh ahl-tersh*
strap alça *f. ahl-ser*
string cordel *m. koor-dehl*
suit (men's) fato (de homem) *m. fah-t^oo (d^e oh-mehn^g)*
suit (women's) fato de saia e casaco *m.*
                  fah-t^oo d^e sahi-er i ker-zah-k^oo
suit (trouser-) fato de calça *m. fah-t^oo d^e kahl-ser*
suitcase mala *f. mah-ler*
thread linha, fio *f., m.* (*lee-nner, fi^oo*)
tie gravata *f. ghrer-vah-ter*
tights meia-calça *f. me(y)i-er-kahl-ser*
tobacco-pouch bolsa de tabaco *f. boul-ser d^e ter-bah-k^oo*
toy brinquedo *m. breen^g-ke(y)-d^oo*
trousers calças *f. kahl-sersh*
umbrella sombrinha, guarda-chuva *f. m.*
              sohn^g-bree-nner, ghwahr-der-shoo-ver
undies roupa interior *f. rrou-per een^g-t^e-ri-our*
wallet carteira *f. ker.r-te(y)i-rer*

watch relógio *m.* *rr*^e**-loh**-*zhi-*^{oo}
wool lã *f.* *lahn*^g
writing paper papel de escrever *m.*
    *per-***pehl** *d*^e ^e*sh-kre-***ve(y)r**

I want to buy	Quero comprar
keh-*r*^{oo} *kohn*^g**-prahr**	
Will you show me some . . .?	Mostre-me uns *m.* umas *f . . .* por favor
mohsh-*tr*^e*-m*^e *oongsh . . .*	**oo-mersh** . . . *, pour fer-***vour**
Have you anything cheaper (dearer)?	Tem alguma coisa mais barata (mais cara)?
tehn^g *ahl-***ghoo-***mer* **koui-***zer* *mahish* *ber-***rah-***ter* (*mahish* **kah-***rer*)?	
Have you anything bigger (smaller)?	Tem maior (mais pequeno)?
tehn^g *mer.i-***ohr** (*mahish* *p*^e**-ke(y)-***n*^{oo})?	
Do you have it in other colours?	Tem outras cores?
tehn^g **ou-***trersh* **kou-***r*^e*sh*	
Can you match this colour?	Tem uma cor que diga bem com esta?
tehn^g **oo-mer** *kour* *ke* **dee-***gher* *behng* *kohng* **ehsh-***ter*?	
Will you deliver it (them)?	Pode mandar a casa?
*poh-***d*^e *mahn*^g**-dahr** *er* *kah-***zer**?	
I will collect it later	Venho buscar mais tarde
ve(y)-*nn*^{oo} *boosh-***kahr** *mahish* **tahr-***d*^e	
That's what I want	Isso é precisamente o que eu quero
ee-*s*^{oo} *eh* *pr*^e*-see-zer-***me(y)n**^g*-t*^e *oo* *k*^e *eh*^{oo} **keh-***r*^{oo}	

It is not suitable Não serve
  nah°°ng **sehr-***v*^{e}

Could you put it (them) in Pode metê-lo (-la, -los, -las)
a box for me? numa caixa, por favor?
  poh-*d*^{e} *m*^{e}**-te(y)-***l*^{oo} (*-ler, -loosh, -lersh*) **noo-***mer* **kahi-***sher,*
  *poor fer-***vour***?*

May I have a receipt? Dê-me um recibo, por
  favor
  de(y)-m^e *oon*^{g} *rr*^{e}**-see-b**^{oo}, *poor fer-***vour**

Can you let me have it Estará pronto (pronta) no
by . . . ? dia . . . ? (Posso vir buscar
  no dia . . .)
  ^{e}**sh-***ter-rah* **prohn**^{g}**-t**^{oo} (**prohn**^{g}**-***ter*) *n*^{oo} *dee-er* . . . ?
  (**poh-***s*^{oo} *veer boosh-***kahr** *n*^{oo} *dee-er* . . . ?)

May I try it (them)? Posso provar?
  poh-*s*^{oo} *proo-***vahr***?*

Can you repair this? Pode consertar isto?
  poh-*d*^{e} *kohn*^{g}**-s**^{e}*r-***tahr** *eesh-***t**^{oo} ?

Can you have it invisibly Pode ser serzido?
mended?
  poh-*d*^{e} *se(y)r* *s*^{e}*r-***zee-d**^{oo} ?

How long will it take? Quando estará pronto?
  kwahn^g**-d**^{oo} ^{e}**sh-***ter-rah* **prohn**^{g}**-t**^{oo} ?

THE CHEMIST

aspirin aspirina *f.* *ersh-pee-***ree-***ner*
bath salts sais de banho *m.* *sahish d*^{e} **ber-***nn*^{oo}
cotton wool algodão *m.* *ahl-ghoo-***dah**^{oo}*n*^{g}
cough mixture xarope para a tosse *m.*
  *sher-***roh-***p*^{e} *per-rer er toh-s*^{e}

79

gargle gargarejo *m. gher.r-gher-***re(y)***-zh⁰⁰*

laxative laxativo *m. ler-sher-tee-*v⁰⁰

lipstick baton *m.* **bah-***tohnᵍ*

medicine medicamento (remédio) *m.*
    *mᵉ-dee-ker-***me(y)***nᵍ-t⁰⁰* (*rre-meh-di-⁰⁰*)

nail file lima de unhas *f.* **lee-***mer dᵉ* **oo-***nnersh*

ointment pomada *f.* **poo-mah-***der*

plaster adesivo (penso rápido) *m.*
    *er-dᵉ-zee-*v⁰⁰ (**pe(y)***nᵍ-s⁰⁰* **rrah-***pee-d⁰⁰*)

powder (face) pó-de-arroz *m. poh dᵉ er-***rroush**

razor blades lâminas (de barbear) *f*
    ler-*mee-nersh dᵉ ber.r-bi-ahr*

sanitary towels pensos higiénicos *m.*
    pe(y)*nᵍ-s⁰⁰s i-zhee-eh-nee-k⁰⁰sh*

scissors tesoura *f. tᵉ-***zou-***rer*

soap sabão (sabonete) *m. ser-***bah⁰⁰**ng (*ser-b⁰⁰-***ne(y)***-te*)

sun glasses óculos para o sol *m.*
    oh-*k⁰⁰-loosh* **per-***rer oo sohl*

sun-tan lotion loção de bronzear *f.*
    *loo-***sahoon***ᵍ dᵉ brohn-zi-ahr*

talcum powder talco *m.* **tahl-***k⁰⁰*

throat pastilles pastilhas para a garganta *f.*
    *persh-***tee-***llersh* **per-***rer er gher.r-***ghahn***ᵍ-ter*

toilet paper papel higiénico *m. per-***pehl** *i-zhee-eh-nee-k⁰⁰*

tooth brush escova de dentes *f.*
    *ᵉsh-***kou-***ver dᵉ* **de(y)***nᵍ-tᵉsh*

tooth paste pasta de dentes *f.* **pahsh-***ter dᵉ* **de(y)***nᵍ-tesh*

Can you make up this prescription?	Pode aviar-me esta receita, por favor?

poh-*dᵉ er-vee-***ahr-***mᵉ* **ehsh-***ter rᵉ-***se(y)***i-ter, poor fer-***vour***?*

Could you let me have   Pode dar-me qualquer
something for . . . ?   coisa para . . . ?
   poh-*d^e* **dahr**-*m^e* **kwahl**-**kehr** koui-*zer* per-*rer . . . ?*

Upset stomach. Headache. Indisposição de estômago.
Dor de cabeça.
*eeng-d^{e}sh-poo-zee-***sah**^{oo}**ng** *d^e* ^{e}*sh-***tou**-*mer-ghoo. dour d^e*
          *ker-***be**(**y**)-*ser.*

Indigestion. Toothache. Indigestão. Dor de dentes.
   *eeng-d^e-zh^{e}sh-***tahoon**^{g}. *dour d^e* **de**(**y**)n^g-*tesh.*

Diarrhoea. Diarreia. *dee-er-***rre**(**y**)i-*er*

I have been sunburnt   Queimei-me ao sol
   ke(*y*)*i-***me**(**y**)**i**-*m^e ah^{oo} sohl*

My feet are blistered   Tenho bolhas nos pés
   te(*y*)*-nn^{oo} bou-***llersh** *n^{oo}sh pehsh*

I want something for insect Arranje-me qualquer coisa
bites   para uma mordedura de
   insecto, por favor
*er-***rrahn**^{g}*-ah^e-m^e kwahl-***kehr** **koui**-*zer* per-*rer* **oo**-*mer*
*moor-di-***doo**-*rer d^e een^g-***seh**-*t^{oo}, poor fer-***vour**

I think it is poisoned   Creio que está infectado
   (infectada)
   kre(**y**)**i**-^{oo} *k^e* ^{e}*sh-***tah** *een^g-feh-***tah**-*doo (een^g-feh-***tah**-*der*)

I have a head cold   Tenho uma constipação
   te(*y*)*-nn^{oo}* **oo**-*mer kohngsh-tee-per-***sah**^{oo}**ng**

My throat is very sore   Tenho a garganta inflamada
   te(*y*)*-nn^{oo} er gher.r-***ghahn**^{g}-*ter een^g-fler-***mah**-*der*

HAIRDRESSER

appointment hora marcada *f.* **oh**-*rer mer.r-***kah**-*der*

bleach oxigenar *oh-ksee-zh^e-nahr*
brush pentear (desembaraçar com escova)
    pe(y)n^g-ti-ahr (d^e-zehn^g-ber-rer-sahr kohn^g
    esh-kou-ver)
colour rinse lavagem de côr f. *ler-vah-zhehn^g d^e kour*
comb pentear *pe(y)n^g-ti-ahr*
cut cortar *koor-tahr*
manicure manicure f. *mah-nee-koo-r^e*
perm permanente f. *p^{e}r-mer-ne(y)n^g-t^e*
set mise f. *mee-z^e*
shampoo shampoo m. (lavagem)
    shahn^g-poo (ler-vah-zhehn^g)
tint pintar (tingir) *peen-tahr (teen^g-zheer)*

May I make an appointment?	Pode marcar-me uma hora?
	pol-d^e mer.r-kahr-m^e oo-mer oh-rer?
I want a shave	Quero fazer a barba
	keh-r^{oo} fer-ze(y)r er bahr-ber
I want a haircut	Quero cortar o cabelo
	keh-r^{oo} koor-tahr oo ker-be(y)-l^{oo}
Not too short	Não muito curto
	nah^{oo}ng mooin^g-t^{oo} koor-t^{oo}
I would like it short	Curto, por favor
	koor-t^{oo}, poor fer-vour
I want a shampoo and set	Quero lavar e pentear
	keh-r^{oo} ler-vahr i pe(y)n^g-ti-ahr
It is too hot (cold)	Está demasiado quente (fria)
	^{e}sh-tah d^e-mer-zee-ah-d^{oo} ke(y)n^g-t^e (free-er)

It is not dry Não está sêco
nah°°nᵍ ᵉsh-**tah se(y)-***k°°*

That is excellent Está óptimo
ᵉsh-**tah oh-***tee-m°°*

THE PHOTOGRAPHIC SHOP

black and white film película preto-branco *f.*
pᵉ-**lee-***k°°-ler* **pre(y)-***t°°-i*-**brahn***ᵍ-k°°*
camera máquina fotográfica *f.*
*mah-kee-ner foo-too-*ghrah-***fee-ker*
colour film película a cores *f.* (rolo de . . .) *m.*
pᵉ-**lee-***k°°-ler er* **kou-***resh (rrou-l°° dᵉ . . .)*
develop revelar *rrᵉ-vᵉ-***lahr**
enlarge ampliar *ahnᵍ-plee-***ahr**
enlargement ampliação *f. ahnᵍ-plee-er-*sah°°ng
exposure-meter tabulador de exposição *m.*
*ter-boo-ler-*dour *dᵉ aysh-p°°-zee-*sah°°nᵍ
filter filtro *m.* feel-*tr°°*
glossy esmaltado *m. esh-mahl-*tah-*d°°*
lens lente (objectiva) *f* le(y)nᵍ-*tᵉ (oh-bzheh-*tee-*ver)*
lens-hood parassol (de objectiva) *m.*
*pah-rer-*sohl *(dᵉ oh-bzheh-*tee-*ver)*
matt sem brilho (neutro) *sehnᵍ* bree-*ll°° (ne(y)°°-tr°°)*
negative negativo *m. nᵉ-gher-*tee-*v°°*
print cópia (prova) *f.* koh-*pi-er* (proh-*ver)*
to print imprimir *inᵍ-pree-*meer
range-finder telémetro *m. tᵉ-*leh-*mᵉ-tr°°*
shutter obturador *m. ohb-too-rer-*dour
view-finder visor *m. vee-*zour
tripod tripé *m.* tree-**peh**

Will you develop (and print) this film?	Façam favor de revelar (e imprimir) esta película (este rolo)?

*fah-sah⁰ oo fer-**vour** dᵉ rrᵉ-vᵉ-**lahr** (i eeng-pree-**meer**) ehsh-ter pᵉ-lee-kᵒᵒ-ler (e(y)sh-tᵉ rrou-lᵒᵒ)?*

I would like some enlargements	Quero ampliações

keh-rᵒᵒ ahn⁰-plee-er-souin⁰sh

When will they be ready?	Quando estarão prontas?

kwahng-dᵒᵒ ᵉsh-ter-rah⁰⁰n⁰ prohn⁰-tersh?

There is something wrong with my camera	Há qualquer coisa que não funciona bem, na minha máquina

*ah kwahl-**kehr** coui-zer kᵉ nah⁰⁰n⁰ fᵒᵒn⁰-see-**oh**-ner behn⁰ ner mee-nner mah-kee-ner*

The film won't turn	A película não roda

er pᵉ-lee-kᵒᵒ-ler nah⁰⁰ng rroh-der

The Beach

Portugal claims to have 580 miles of beach, and it is fair to say that a great proportion of her coastline is indeed sandy and suitable for bathing. The map shows some 130 recognised resorts, but of course there are many more places tucked away out of sight of the milling throngs that will doubtless invade them soon.

Most beaches in the more popular areas have relaxed their views on bikinis, but in places where tourists are a novelty it is best to wear a one-piece swimsuit. Shorts –

for women – are not always acceptable, either. Doubtless it will not be long before such attempts to preserve female modesty are abandoned!

USEFUL WORDS AND PHRASES

bathe banhar-se *ber-nnahr-s^e*
bathing cabin barraca de praia *f.*
        ber-rrah-ker-d^e **prahi**-*er*
bathing cap touca de banho *f.* **tou**-*ker d^e* **ber-nn**^{oo}
bathing costume fato de banho *m.* **fah**-*t^{oo} d^e* **ber-nn**^{oo}
bay baía *f.* **ber-ee**-*er*
beach praia *f.* **prahi**-*er*
boat barco *m.* **bahr**-*k^{oo}*
buoy boia *f.* **bohi**-*er*
canoe canoa *f.* **ker-nou**-*er*
cliff falésia *f.* *fer-leh-zi*-*er*
coast costa *f.* **kohsh**-*ter*
current corrente *f.* *k^{oo}-rre(y)n^g-t^e*
deck chair cadeira de convés *f.*
        ker-de(y)i-rer d^e **kohn**^{g}-*vehsh*
diving board prancha de saltos *f.*
        prahn^g-*sher d^e* **sahl**-*t^{oo}sh*
fish peixe *m.* **pe(y)i**-*sh^e*
to fish pescar *p^{e}sh*-**kahr**
flippers barbatanas *f.* *ber.r-ber-ter-nersh*
jelly-fish alforreca *f.* *ahl-f^{oo}*-**rreh**-*ker*
pebbles seixos, pedras *f.* *se(y)i-sh^{oo}sh,* **peh**-*drersh*
raft jangada *f.* *zhahn^g-ghah-der*
rocks rochas (pedras) *f.* **rroh**-*shersh* (**peh**-*drersh*)
sand areia *f.* *er-re(y)i*-*er*
sandhills dunas *f.* **doo**-*nersh*

shell concha *f.* **kohn***ᵍ-sher*
snorkel respirador aquático *m.*
    *rrᵉsh-pee-rer-***dour** *er-***kwah***-tee-kᵒᵒ*
sunshade toldo (parassol, sombrinha) *m.* (*m., f.*)
    toul*-dᵒᵒ* (*pah-rer-***sohl**, *sohnᵍ-***bree***-nner*)
tide maré *f.* **mer***-reh*
water skis skis aquáticos (esquis) *m.*
    *sᵉ-***keesh** *er-***kwah***-tee-koosh-*(*esh-***keesh**)
wave onda *f.* **ohn***ᵍ-der*

Which is the way to the beach?	Qual é o caminho para a praia?

    *kwahl eh oo ker-***mee***-nnᵒᵒ* **per***-r' ah* **prahi***-er*?

Can I hire a deck-chair (sunshade, cabin)?	Posso alugar uma cadeira de convés (toldo, barraca)?

poh*-sᵒᵒ er-loo-***ghahr** *oo-mer ker-***de***(y)i-rer dᵉ* **kohn***ᵍ-*
    vehsh (**toul***-dᵒᵒ*, *ber-***rrah***-ker*?)

Can I hire some flippers?	Posso alugar umas barbatanas?

poh*-sᵒᵒ er-loo-***ghahr** *oo-mersh ber.r-ber-***ter***-nersh*?

Can I hire a snorkel?	Posso alugar um respirador?

poh*-sᵒᵒ er-loo-***ghahr** *oong rrᵉsh-pee-rer-***dour**?

Where is it safe to bathe?	Onde se pode tomar banho?

ohn*ᵍ-dᵉ sᵉ* **poh***-dᵉ too-***mahr** *ber-***nnᵒᵒ**?

Can I go fishing?	Posso ir à pesca?

poh*-sᵒᵒ eer ah* **pehsh***-ker*?

I am not a good swimmer	Não sei nadar muito bem

nahᵒᵒng se(*y*)*i ner-***dahr** *mooinᵍ-tᵒᵒ* **behn***ᵍ*

Bathing prohibited	Proibido nadar

*proo-ee-bee-dᵒᵒ ner-***dahr**

Can I hire a sailing boat (rowing, motor boat)?	Posso alugar um barco à vela (barco a remos, barco a motor)?

  poh-*s^{oo}* er-*loo*-**ghahr** *oong* **bahr**-*k^{oo}* ah veh-*ler*
  (**bahr**-*k^{oo}* er reh-*moosh*, **bahr**-*k^{oo}* er moo-**tour**) *?*

Where can I go water-skiing?	Onde se pode fazer o ski aquático?

  ohn^e-*d^e* s^e poh-*d^e* fer-ze(y)r *oo* s^e-**kee** er-kwah-*tee-koo* *?*

I only want to sunbathe	Só quero apanhar sol

  soh keh-*r^{oo}* er-per-*nnahr sohl*

Is it dangerous?	É perigoso?

  *eh p^e-ree-***ghou**-*z^{oo}* *?*

Are there any rocks here?	Há rochas, por aqui?

  ah roh-*shersh*, *poor* er-**kee***?*

Is there a shower?	Há chuveiros?

  ah shoo-**ve(y)i**-*r^{oo}sh* *?*

Post Office, Telephone

Post Offices are open from 9 a.m. to 6 p.m. and stamps are also obtainable from tobacconists licensed to sell them (an outside sign is clearly visible). The hotel porter will always have some handy for those who need them quickly. The English-style post boxes are painted red, as are the public telephone kiosks. The telephone system is automatic – which is lucky, as there are few operators who can speak English sufficiently well.

Remember that you will need your passport when collecting "Poste Restante" mail.

USEFUL WORDS AND PHRASES

cablegram cabograma *m.* *kah-b°°-ghrer-mer*
call chamada telefónica *f.* *sher-mah-der t*^e^*-l*^e^*-foh-nee-ker*
collection tiragem (dos correios) *f.*
    tee-rah-zheng (doosh koo-rre(y)i-oosh)
directory lista dos telefones *f.*
    leesh-ter doosh t^e^*-l*^e^*-foh-n*^e^*sh*
international money order vale postal internacional *m.*
    vah-le poosh-tahl een^a^*-t*^e^*r-*
    ner-see-°°*-nahl*
letter carta *f.* *kahr-ter*
letter box marco do correio (caixa postal) *m.* (*f.*)
    mahr-k°° *doo koo-rre(y)i-*°°
    (*kahi-sher poosh-tahl*)
post card postal *m.* *poosh-tahl*
post office estação dos correios *f.*
    ^e^*sh-ter-sah*°°*ng doosh koo-rre(y)i-oosh*
postal order vale postal, *m.* *vah-l*^e^ *poosh-tahl*
number número *m.* *noo-m*^e^*-r*°°
to register registar *re-zheesh-tahr*
stamp selo *m.* *se(y)-l*°°
telegram telegrama *m.* *t*^e^*-l*^e^*-ghrer-mer*
telephone telefone *m.* *t*^e^*-l*^e^*-foh-n*^e^
to telephone telefonar *t*^e^*-l*^e^*-foo-nahr*
telephone box cabina telefónica *f.*
    kah-bee-ner t^e^*-l*^e^*-foh-nee-ker*

Where is the nearest post office? Onde é o correio mais próximo?
    ohn^a^*-d*^e^ *eh oo ko-rre(y)i-oo mahish proh-see-m*°° *?*

I want to send this post card (letter)	Quero enviar este postal (esta carta)
keh-*r*ᵒᵒ *e(y)n*ᵍ-*vi*-ahr *e(y)sh*-*t*ᵉ poosh-**tahl** (ehsh-*ter* kahr-*ter*)	
I want to send this parcel	Quero enviar esta encomenda postal
keh-*r*ᵒᵒ *e(y)n*ᵍ-*vi*-ahr ehsh-*ter e(y)n*ᵍ-*k*ᵒᵒ-**me(y)n**ᵍ-*der* poosh-**tahl**	
I want to register this letter	Quero registar esta carta
keh-*r*ᵒᵒ *rr*ᵉ-*zheesh*-**tahr** ehsh-*ter* kahr-*ter*	
Are there any letters for me?	Tem algum correio para . . . ?
*tehn*ᵍ ahl-**ghoong** koo-**rre(y)i**-ᵒᵒ per-rer . . . ?	
Is there a parcel for me?	Alguma encomenda para mim?
ahl-**ghoo**-mer *e(y)n*ᵍ-*k*ᵒᵒ-**me(y)n**ᵍ-*der* per-rer meenᵍ ?	
Here is my passport	Aqui tem o meu passaporte
er-**kee** tehnᵍ oo mehᵒᵒ pah-ser-**pohr**-tᵉ	

Medical Services

There is as yet no reciprocal National Health agreement between Britain and Portugal and you will have to pay for any hospital treatment necessary during your stay. This applies as well to chemists' prescriptions, which might otherwise be cheaper, and also to doctors' and dentists' consultation fees. So it is most important to

take out an insurance policy against being ill while on
holiday.

If you are worried about drinking water, it is not
a bad idea to stick to the various mineral waters that
are generally available; they'll do you no more harm
than the ordinary water (which is probably alright) and
you'll enjoy your holiday more.

USEFUL WORDS AND PHRASES

accident desastre, acidente *m.*
      *d^e-***zahsh**-*tr^e*, *er-see-***de(y)n^g**-*t^e*
ambulance ambulância *f.* *ahn^g-boo-***lahn^g***-see-er*
appendicitis apêndice, apendicite *m., f.*
      *er-***pe(y)n^g***-d^e-s^e*, *er-pe(y)n^g-d^e-***see***-t^e*
bandage ligadura *f.* *lee-gher-***doo**-*rer*
bite mordidela, picada *f.* *moor-dee-***deh**-*ler*, *pee-***kah**-*der*
blister bolha *f.* **bou**-*ller*
burn queimadura *f.* *ke(y)i-mer-***doo**-*rer*
chill resfriamento *m.* *rr^esh-free-er-***me(y)n^g**-*t^{oo}*
constipation prisão de ventre *m.*
      *pree-***zah^{oo}ng** *d^e* **ve(y)n^g**-*tre*
cough tosse *f.* *toh-s^e*
to cough tossir *too-***seer**
cramp cãibra *f.* **kahin^g**-*brer*
cut golpe, corte, ferida *m., m., f.*
      ghohl-*p^e*, **kohr**-*t^e*, *f^e-***ree**-*der*
dentist dentista *m.* *de(y)n^g-***teesh**-*ter*
diarrhoea diarreia, soltura *f.*
      *dee-er-***rre(y)i**-*er*, *soul-***too**-*rer*
doctor médico, doutor *m* *meh-***dee**-*k^{oo}*, *dou-***tour**
faint (n) desmaio *m.* *d^esh-***mahi**-*^{oo}*

to faint desmaiar *desh-mahi-ahr*
fever febre *f.* **feh**-*br^e*
fracture fractura *f. frah-too-rer*
hospital hospital *m. ohsh-pee-***tahl**
indigestion indigestão *m. een^g-d^e-zh^esh-***tah**^oo**n**^g
influenza gripe *f* **ghree**-*p^e*
insomnia insónia *f. een^g-soh-ni-er*
injection injecção *f. een^g-zheh-***sah**^oo**n**^g
nurse enfermeira *f. e(y)n^g-f^er-***me(y)i**-*rer*
pain dor *f. dour*
poison veneno *m. v^e-***ne(y)**-*n^oo*
policeman polícia, guarda *m. p^oo-lee-si-er,* **ghwahr**-*der*
sling suporte de braço-ao-peito *m.*
    *s^oo-***pohr**-*t^e d^e* **brah**-*s^oo-ah^oo-***pe(y)i**-*t^oo*
sprain distenção, torcedura *f.*
    *d^esh-te(y)n^g-***sah**^oo**ng**, *toor-s^e-***doo**-*rer*
sting picada, picadela *f. pee-***kah**-*der, pee-ker-***deh**-*ler*
stomach ache dor de estômago *f.*
    *dour d^e ^esh-tou-mer-***gh**^oo
sunstroke insolação *f. een^g-soo-ler-***sah**^oo**ng**
surgery consultório, clínica *m., f.*
    *kohn^g-sool-***toh**-*ri-^oo,* **klee**-*nee-ker*
temperature febre, temperatura *f.*
    feh-*bre, te(y)n^g-p^e-rer-too-rer*
throat garganta (*f.*) *gher.r-***ghahn**^g-*ter*
toothache dor de dentes *f. dour d^e* **de(y)n**^g-*t^esh*
vomit vómitos *m. voh-***mee**-*t^oosh*

Call an ambulance quickly Chame uma ambulância,
                            depressa
    sher-*m^e* **oo**-*mer ahn^g-boo-***lahn**^g-*si-er d^e-***preh**-*ser*

Call a policeman quickly Chame um polícia,
depressa
*sher-m^e oon^g poo-lee-si-er d^e-**preh**-ser*

Stand back Afaste-se (afastem-se)
*er-**fahsh**-t^e-s^e (er-**fahsh**-tehn^g-s^e)*

Give him (her) air Dêem-lhe ar (Deixem-no
(-na) respirar)
*de(y)-ehn^g-lle ahr (de(y)i-shehn^g-n^oo (-ner) rr^esh-peer-**rahr**)*

Do not move him (her) Não o (a) movam
nah^oong oo (er) mou-vah^ong

Is there a doctor near here? Há um médico perto daqui?
*ah oong meh-dee-k^oo pehr-t^oo der-**kee**?*

Have you a bandage? Tem uma ligadura?
*tehn^g oo-mer lee-gher-**doo**-rer?*

I have a pain here Doi-me aqui
*dohi-m^e er-**kee***

Bring some hot (cold) water Traga água quente (fria)
*trah-gher ah-ghwer ke(y)n^g-t^e (**free**-er)*

Bring me a blanket Traga-me uma manta
(um cobertor)
*trah-gher-m^e oo-mer mahn^g-ter (oong koo-b^er-**tour**)*

I am feeling very ill Sinto-me muito mal
(muito doente)
seen^g-t^oo-me mooin^g-t^oo mahl (mooin^g-t^oo d^oo-e(y)n^g-t^e)

Please bring a doctor Chamem um médico,
por favor
*sher-mehn^g oon^g meh-dee-k^oo, poor fer-**vour***

92

Do you have any pain here?	Doi-lhe aqui?

                  dohi-*ll*^{e} *er-***kee***?*

Where is the nearest dentist?	Onde é o dentista mais próximo?

    ohng-*d*^{e} *eh oo de(y)n*^{g}**-teesh-***ter mahish* **proh-***see-m*^{oo}?

Will you give me an injection?	Dê-me uma injecção, por favor

    de(y)-*m*^{e} *oo-mer een*^{g}**-zheh-***sah*^{oo}*n*^{g}, *poor fer-***vour**

Useful Information

Currency, Banks

The monetary unit is the escudo, written as 1$00. The decimal units (centavos) are popularly known as "tostões". There are coins in the following amounts: 50$00, 20$00, 10$00, 5$00, 2$50, $50, $20 and $10. Written down like this, it looks as if the 50 centavo piece is in fact 50 escudos (or, indeed, 50 dollars); in terms of buying power the lone coin is fairly useless and so you are unlikely to come up against such a confusion. But bear the fact in mind; officially the escudos sign comes *after* the amount in escudos. Notes exist in 1000$00, 500$00, 100$00, 50$00 and 20$00 denominations.

As rates of exchange are subject to fluctuation, we suggest you pencil in the current sterling equivalents below:

1,000$00 = £		50$00 = £	
500$00 = £		20$00 = £	
100$00 = £		10$00 = £	
75$00 = £		1$00 = £	

Banks are open from 9.30 a.m. to noon and from 2 p.m. to 4 p.m. on weekdays; on Saturdays they open from 9.30 a.m. to 11.30 a.m. Some banks in the main tourist areas keep an exchange service open from 6.30 p.m. to 11 p.m. Exchange bureaux are open from 9 a.m. to 1 p.m. and from 3 p.m. to 6 p.m. Monday–Friday, and from 9 a.m. to 1 p.m. on Saturdays.

Tipping

A service charge is usually included in all hotel and restaurant bills – 10%. Further tips are optional (but in most cases welcome!). In cinemas and theatres the tip varies between one and five escudos; 1$00 is usual when you have a cup of coffee, and in bars you should add 10% to the bill. Taxi drivers expect 10%–15%, and railway porters about 2$50 per bag. Ladies' hairdressers are tipped anything between ten and twenty escudos, with 5$00 for the girl who washes your hair. Men should tip their barber 5$00 also.

Conversion Tables

TYRE PRESSURES

lbs. per sq. inch	17	18	19	20
kg. per sq. cm.	1k 200	1k 250	1k 350	1k 400
lbs. per sq. inch	21	22	23	24
kg. per sq. cm.	1k 475	1k 500	1k 600	1k 700
lbs. per sq. inch	25	26	27	28
kg. per sq. cm.	1k 750	1k 850	1k 900	1k 950

DISTANCES

Distances are marked in kilometres To convert kilometres to miles, divide the km. by 8 and multiply by 5. Convert miles to km. by dividing the miles by 5 and multiplying by 8. A mile is 1 km. 610 m.

km.	miles or km.	miles	km.	miles or km.	miles
1·6	1	0·6	16·1	10	6·2
3·2	2	1·2	32·2	20	12·4
4·8	3	1·9	48·3	30	18·6
6·4	4	2·5	64·4	40	24·9
8·1	5	3·1	80·5	50	31·1
9·7	6	3·7	160·9	100	62·1
11·3	7	4·4	321·9	200	124·2
12·9	8	5·0	804·7	500	310·7
14·5	9	5·6	1609·4	1000	621·4

Other units of length

1 centimetre	= 0·39 in.	1 inch	= 25·4 millimetres
1 metre	= 39·37 in.	1 foot	= 0·30 metre (30 cm.)
10 metres	= 32·81 ft.	1 yard	= 0·91 metre

WEIGHTS

The unit you will come into most contact with is the kilogram, or kilo. To convert kg. to lbs., multiply by 2 and add $\frac{1}{10}$ of the result. One kilo (1000 gr.) is 2 lb. 3 oz.; one stone is 6·35 kg.; one cwt. is 51 kg.

grams	**ounces**		ounces		grams
50	1·75		1		28·0
100	3·50		2		57·1
250	8·80		4		114·3
500	17·6		8		228·6

	lbs.			lbs.	
kg.	*or* kg.	lbs.	kg.	*or* kg.	lbs.
0·5	1	2·2	3·6	8	17·6
0·9	2	4·4	4·1	9	19·8
1·4	3	6·6	4·5	10	22·1
1·8	4	8·8	9·1	20	44·1
2·3	5	11·0	11·3	25	55·1
2·7	6	13·2	22·7	50	110·2
3·2	7	15·4	45·4	100	220·5

LIQUIDS

Petrol being sold in litres, the following table (in Imperial gallons) will aid your calculations – remember that while an Imperial gallon is roughly 4½ litres, an American gallon is only 3·8 litres. One litre is about 1¾ pints, a pint is 0·57 litre.

	gals.			gals.	
litres	*or* l.	gals.	litres	*or* l.	gals.
4·6	1	0·2	36·4	8	1·8
9·1	2	0·4	40·9	9	2·0
13·6	3	0·7	45·5	10	2·2
18·2	4	0·9	90·9	20	4·4
22·7	5	1·1	136·4	30	6·6
27·3	6	1·3	181·8	40	8·8
31·8	7	1·5	227·3	50	11·0